# HELL RAISERS

# HELL RAISERS

## Peter Carrick

PELHAM BOOKS

First published in Great Britain by PELHAM BOOKS
52 Bedford Square, London WC1B 3EF
1973

ISBN 0 7207 0668 8

*Set and printed in Great Britain by*
*Tonbridge Printers Ltd, Peach Hall Works, Tonbridge, Kent*
*in Caledonia ten on twelve point on paper supplied by*
*P. F. Bingham Ltd, and bound by James Burn*
*at Esher, Surrey*

# ACKNOWLEDGEMENTS

Many people have helped me with HELL
RAISERS by remembering incidents, offering me
their frank views, and verifying dates, places,
people and situations. I thank them all. In particular I thank those who are the subject of
chapters, and in certain instances their relatives
and friends; the Auto-Cycle Union; the maga-
zines *Motor Cycle News* and *Motor Cycle* from
whose pages much research was completed.

The author is also grateful to Motor Racing
Publications Limited for permission to use an
extract from *No Time To Lose* by Alan Peck,
and to Arthur Barker Limited for permission
to reproduce extracts from *Racing All My Life*
by Derek Minter, *Wheels of Fortune* by Jim
Redman, and *Prince of Speed,* by Phil Read.

# CONTENTS

# Contents

# ILLUSTRATIONS

## Illustrations

15 A closer view of Cooper's remarkable machine

*Between pages 112–113*

ACKNOWLEDGEMENTS

The author's thanks are due to the following, whose photographs are reproduced in this book:
Nick Nicholls: 3, 4, 5, 6, 7, 8, 9, 11, 12, 13, 14, 15, 16, 17, 18, 19, 20, 22;
Dave Dixon: 10.

# Introduction
# 'Put me in the Saddle'

Racing motor cycles is a rugged business. It takes courage to thunder along at 100 mph on two wheels. Tazio Nuvolari was a brave Italian. He raced motor cycles. One remarkable incident from his breathtaking career demonstrates the courage of men who ride motor cycles at speed.

Nuvolari won more than 300 motor cycle races. His most memorable ride was at Monza in 1928. Practising for the Italian Grand Prix he crashed heavily, breaking both legs. The doctors told him he would be in hospital for a month. The next day he was on the starting line, both legs in plaster. Two mechanics had hoisted him into the saddle. Then they tied him to the bike. They held him there until the race started.

'If Nuvolari falls just once,' protested the surgeon, 'he's a dead man. Don't call me. I won't even come. There would be no point in it.'

Nuvolari raced 300 kilometres and won the race. Then he coasted in at 3 mph so that his mechanics could lift him off the machine.

This is the bravery of motor cycle racing. No other sport has savoured so much of the heroism, the 'blood and guts' atmosphere of those dashing pioneering days. Still there remains the old-time personal challenge and adventure. Machines are more powerful and far more complex now. Speeds are twice what they were. Top riders have fashionable haircuts and ten per cent agents.

But skim away the present-day gloss and the sport is the same as it always was – vigorous, gloriously abandoned, reckless, courageous, fast and daring.

Inevitably too, comes disaster. More than thirty years after

11

Nuvolari's astonishing display of personal courage, we look at bravery of a different kind.

Dave Downer and Derek Minter are locked in close combat, racing headlong into tragedy in an exciting display of riding which has the crowd on its toes. Blasting round Brands Hatch at 90 mph Dave has the power to lead on the straights, but Derek, the acknowledged King of Brands, can outride him on the bends. Into the final lap, with Minter taking the lead at Westfield Bend. He is first into Dingle Dell Corner. Then disaster as an almighty crash brings them down. Dave Downer dies.

Minter, his spine fractured, was haunted by the memory of the fatal accident as he lay for weeks in hospital. He had known Downer well. Had raced with him often. Now he was gone and I know that Derek, because of his involvement in the accident, lived for some considerable time with the haunting feeling that somehow he might have been to blame.

Motor cycle racing sorts out the men from the boys. Minter was man enough to live with the spectre of that accident, to race and thrill crowds often in the days that followed.

Life hangs by a thread whenever a racer leaps into the saddle. But the thrill and adventure of being one of the fast ones means more to him than life itself.

Riders are pig-headed and rebellious. They are scarred with the injuries of battle. Because the motor cycle racer does what he does, because he is who he is, you will find he is often a hell raiser. He has to be, in order to raise hell when he hurtles his machine over the tarmac.

You can not change the breed. Who would want to?

# 1
# Ten Tempestuous Years

The 'sixties constituted the most sensational period in the history of motor cycle racing. The Japanese factories launched themselves dramatically on the international circuits. With big-money contracts, they wooed the top British riders ... and won almost every major title. Then, as dramatically as they had arrived, they left.

It was a decade when Mike Hailwood became the greatest name motor cycle racing has known. The Swinging 'sixties, for the first time in history, gave a glamour image to a completely new style of luxury-living, pop-style motor cycle road racer from Britain – money-conscious, flower-powered, long-haired, and internationally successful. For this new style super-star it became a world of jet-set travel, West End luxury flats, dolly girl followers, hectic parties, fast moving cars and, above all, fat works contracts to pay for it all.

The period produced the sport's most volatile riders and some of the greatest dramas, both on and off the track. There were bitter feuds, major controversies, stupid fights and squabbles, organised opposition to authority.

As machinery improved and speeds increased it was also a time of great daring and courage, skilful and devastating riding. It was a hard world filled with tough, unyielding characters who projected a reckless, materialistic approach to life. They freely admitted that money meant most. They knew their worth to racing factories bent on world honours and weren't afraid to state their price.

There was a racing ban for Dave Degens: death at high speed for incredible characters like Bill Ivy, John Hartle and Fritz Scheidegger. It was a time of domestic tragedy, sensational crashes and unjust disqualifications. It was a time when

Greenwood's mini-racer, which was based on the Mini Cooper car, angered many fans and some riders. It was a time of a British world-beater that backfired. Times were stirring and deeds heroic. The 'sixties stretched from McIntyre to Agostini, from Ubbiali to Read, from Surtees to Hailwood. The period was a treasure chest of talent, a bonanza of brilliant riding.

Yet curiously, the 'sixties started dismally. John Surtees, after his exceptional success on motor cycles, was about to move into car racing. Carlo Ubbiali, one of Italy's most brilliant riders, was soon to retire, and the domination in world side-car racing of BMW and Max Deubel was yet to move into full stride.

Most depressing of all was that Guzzi and Gilera, who with MV had filled the 'fifties with spectacular racing, had already retired from racing because of the crippling costs of Grand Prix participation and a dwindling home market for motor bikes.

Nineteen-Sixty brought the last world titles for Ubbiali, who gained his third successive success for MV in the 125 cc and made it two in a row, again for MV, in the 250 cc category; and for John Surtees who, in 1960, completed a hat-trick of world victories in the 350 cc and 500 cc classes, also on MV machinery.

But glorious, speed-packed days were just around the corner. At home McIntyre was to thrill us for two more years before his fatal crash, and Minter was approaching his prime. Abroad, the world classics were soon to witness the vintage racing of Hailwood, Agostini, Ivy, Read, Taveri, Anderson, Redman, and others.

Most important of all, the Japanese were about to enter motor cycle racing at an international level, with a big ambition and fine machinery. Strange sounding names like Yamaha, Suzuki and, above all, Honda, were to dominate the racing scene, as Norton and Matchless had done in the 'thirties, and for the same reason: phenomenal success!

Honda's racing years were to be as dramatic and devastating as anything seen before or since. Their success was to constitute one of the most illustrious chapters in the history of motor cycle sport, with 18 world championships and 137 classic victories.

Honda had been a force at home before they started racing in Europe. They spread their wings with a potentially lucrative commercial market as the basis of their interest. They contested the TT for the first time in 1959 with a team of three Japanese riders. Though failing to secure individual honours, they won immediate distinction when they became the first foreign factory to win the team prize, following their sixth, seventh and eleventh placings in the 125 cc event.

This brief look outside Japan convinced Honda of the superiority of foreign riders and the following year they signed Tom Phillis and Jim Redman. In 1960 they were unsuccessful in the World Championships. How different twelve months later. In 1961 Tom Phillis of Australia rode a Honda to become World 125 cc Champion, and Mike Hailwood of Britain rode a Honda to become World 250 cc Champion. And in the TT Races of 1961 Honda secured the first three places in both the 125 and 250 cc events.

For the remainder of the 'sixties the Japanese, spearheaded by the Honda assault, dominated the world classics in all but the 500 cc and sidecar events. The 50 cc class started in 1962 with a world victory for Ernst Degner of West Germany on a Suzuki. The same factory, with New Zealand's Hugh Anderson riding, secured the title again in 1963 and 1964. Ralph Bryans of Ireland on a Honda became World 50 cc Champion in 1965, but Suzuki won the title for the next three years, with machines piloted by West Germany's Hans-Georg Anscheidt. The run was broken in 1969 when the title went to Nieto of Spain on a Derbi.

In the 125 cc World Championship the Japanese swept through uninterrupted from 1961. It was Honda in '61 and '62, Suzuki in '63, Honda in '64, Suzuki again in '65, Honda '66 and then Yamaha, with first Bill Ivy and then Phil Read, in '67 and '68. Dave Simmonds on a Kawasaki completed Japan's domination during the 'sixties.

There was parallel achievement in the 250 cc World championship. With Hailwood, Redman and Read, Japanese Hondas and Yamahas gained every Championship from 1961 to 1968, Kel Carruthers of Australia on a Benelli clinching the title in 1969. In the 350 cc World Championship Honda, first with Redman and then with Hailwood, had a clear run of victories from 1962 to 1967.

Glowing with national pride Honda set about an assault on the Senior class. At this time MV had both Hailwood and Agostini riding for them. Honda bid for the top and tempted Mike Hailwood with a big-money contract.

Now the battle of the giants was on with a vengeance. With the 500 cc World Title in their possession Honda could retire from racing having beaten Britain and the rest of the world at their own game.

But it was not to be. Although Hailwood brought home the Senior TT for Honda, handling problems on the big machine, which led to Mike's often bristling relationship with the Honda camp, were never overcome and Honda left the international arena with their most cherished ambition, sadly, unfulfilled. Injustice indeed for all that Honda had done for motor cycle racing.

At the start of the 'sixties BMW had already become something of a legend in the 500 cc sidecar World Championship. They had gained every title since 1954, twice with Wellhelm Noll in '54 and '56, then with Wellhelm Faust in '55, Fritz Hillebrand ('57) and Walter Schneider ('58 and '59), all of West Germany. We watched wide-eyed and open-mouthed as the incredible reliability of the BMW sustained the German factory's outright domination throughout the 'sixties. BMW almost all the way: Helmut Fath (1960), Max Deubel (1961, 1964), Fritz Scheidegger (1965 and 1966), Klaus Enders (1967), and Klaus Enders again in 1969. It was the most firmly-entrenched class domination in contemporary road racing – a modern miracle.

Although the World Championships captured the greatest attention, the 'sixties brought a number of milestones nearer home. At the Isle of Man, the magic 100 mph lap, first achieved by Bob McIntyre in 1957 on a Gilera, was only equalled twice in 1958 and once in 1959, by John Hartle (once) and John Surtees (twice). In 1960 the 100 mph lap was raced no fewer than twelve times by Surtees, Hartle, Hailwood and Minter. Mrs Beryl Swain created a sensation in 1962 when she became the first female ever to take part in the TT Races, finishing in 22nd position in the 50 cc event on an Itom. A year earlier every one of the 45 finishers in the Senior TT rode British machines. In 1967 the TT Races celebrated their Diamond

Jubilee, with a number of special events organised for the occasion.

It was in the 'sixties too that MV became invincible in the 500 cc World Championship. With the Honda and Hailwood challenge swept aside there was nothing to stop the MV, with Agostini aboard, from thundering from one outstanding triumph to another. Results became predictable. Agostini was faced with riding against himself and against the clock in race after race.

The irony of it all was that Mike Hailwood had earlier succeeded with MV where he later failed with Honda. In 1962, again in 1963, yet again in 1964 and once more in 1965, Mike rushed to World victories in the 500 cc class on the MV. But in the mid-'sixties the brilliant and handsome Agostini was blossoming into a rider of exceptional skill, daring and merit.

It was Agostini's professional challenge to Mike's 'top dog' position which Hailwood preferred not to accept, claimed his critics. Mike said he shifted to Honda because they offered him more money. But he must also have felt he had a good chance of capturing the 500 cc World Title for the Japanese factory, and was obviously attracted by the massive effort Honda were prepared to make to gain it.

Agostini immediately became a formidable rival to Mike, and in the end a larger version of the three-cylinder 350 which Mike himself had helped to develop, proved too good for the unreliable Honda.

The handling problems of the four-cylinder Honda 500 which had cost Mike the title in 1966 persisted in 1967. The Honda could go fast enough, but, Mike just couldn't keep it going long enough! In the Isle of Man Mike rode well in spite of trouble from a loose twist grip. For most of the race victory for Agostini seemed certain, but a broken chain with little more than a lap to go, let Mike through to take the race.

In Holland Hailwood had things going for him from the start. He cleaned up in the 250 and 350 events, and for the opening laps of the 500 was content to follow Agostini round at close range. Then he surged ahead and in a supreme example of sheer determination and riding skill was first home.

Hailwood went to contest the Belgium GP at Spa two-to-one up in the World Championship. A victory there would give him a tremendous psychological advantage over his arch rival. But the Honda again let him down. After a bad start Mike found the machine too difficult to handle at speed and Agostini on the more manageable MV went on to win. In East Germany Agostini went three-two up as a furious Mike suffered a broken gearbox.

The battle raged, first one race going to Agostini, the next to Hailwood. They approached Monza for an Italian Grand Prix that would decide the World Championship. Each had scored the same number of wins and at the start Mike went relentlessly after the kill. He stormed in front of Agostini with such power that he outpaced the previous lap record by 3 mph. At this point you could have bet on a Honda/Hailwood victory. Then the Honda stuck in sixth gear and Agostini went on to take the title.

Hailwood retired in 1969 to go car racing. He had won a dozen TT races, two more than any other rider, and shared with Carlo Ubbiali the record of nine world titles. But on the Honda he was never able to wrestle the 500 cc World Championship title from the MV and Agostini.

In a phenomenal career Mike Hailwood's greatest achievements were recorded during the golden days of the 'sixties. Winning the Senior TT is tough enough. The way Mike did it in 1965 was sheer drama. He crashed, discovered he was unhurt, picked himself up, got the MV going again, climbed aboard, and went on to win.

These were the stirring deeds which made motor cycle racing history in the 'sixties. Deeds, too, like Hailwood's remarkable visit to Daytona when he scored two shattering successes in the space of 24 hours. What a day! In the morning of that special Hailwood day in 1964, he broke the world one-hour record at 144 mph and in the afternoon raced to victory in the United States 500 cc Grand Prix.

Bob McIntyre had put up the world one-hour record seven years before at Monza on a Gilera at 143 mph. Mike's first lap came out at only 136.5 mph, far short of the record. After 15 minutes he was lapping at more than 146 mph and had hauled up the average to 141. With half the race gone he was still falling short at only 142.9 mph, but he was within reach of the record. A few more laps and Hailwood was going round at

more than 145, but then his MV began to lose speed, a second
on one lap, two on the next. He stretched every yard of performance out of the bike to take the record at 144.8 mph.

With the excitement and fatigue of the world record behind
him Hailwood was in the saddle again in the afternoon, facing
a further gruelling 127 miles of racing against tough opposition.
Yet again he was a record breaker. For fourteen laps there was
little between Hailwood and Caldarella on a Gilera. These two
had stormed so far ahead of the opposition that when Caldarella
had to retire with gear-box trouble, Mike not only rode on to
win, but set up new race and lap records at 100.16 mph and
103.3 mph respectively. It was a remarkable achievement and
brought Hailwood once more into the headlines.

It is staggering how often Mike was in the news. He figured
prominently in much that added up to motor cycle racing in
the 'sixties. Of course, he suffered at the hands of critics who
enjoyed the prospect of seeing him knocked from the privileged
perch his millionaire father had created for him. He had had the
money. He had had the support. He had bought the best bikes.
Those who were fond of seeing Mike struggling relished his
luckless fight against Agostini and MV towards the end of his
motor bike career. They had rubbed their hands in glee once
before, but the sight of the mighty Mike down on his luck was
denied them. This was in 1963 when, through an enterprising
move by Geoffrey Duke, the fabulous 1957 Gileras were once
again wheeled out after being six years under dust covers in
the Italian marque's factory.

MV had already established a five year monopoly of the
world 500 cc championship, with Mike Hailwood collecting his
first MV Senior world title just a year before. When Duke
selected Derek Minter and John Hartle as his riders great
battles were anticipated for 1963.

Derek had said he was more than a match for Mike on equal
machinery. Now was his chance to prove it. If the Gilera's
were up to performance, 1963 could produce some really
spectacular racing. Hartle and Minter went to Monza to test
the Gileras. We excitedly awaited their verdict. Tension rose
high when we read about the speeds of the Gileras. As Derek
reported later in his book *Racing All My Life*: 'Those first
tests were little short of sensational. By golly could those Gilera

fours still go. Before the three-day tests were over both John and myself were lapping consistently at around the 116 mph mark, and I came within a fraction of breaking John Surtees' Monza lap record, which he had set up on an MV four, as I hurtled round at over 118 mph. And my time was faster than a Gilera had ever previously been raced round the Monza circuit – ahead of the 118.04 mph set up by the late Libero Liberati when winning the 1957 Italian Grand Prix.'

When Derek and John romped home first and second at the Silverstone meeting early in the season, it seemed the Gileras were all set for a glorious comeback under the Geoffrey Duke banner.

The initial battle between Minter and Hailwood should have taken place at Brands Hatch where a record 60,000 crowd turned out to see the tussle. But a fall in an earlier event prevented Mike from competing, though Minter's Gileras showed their paces by thundering to success in both the 500 cc and 1000 cc events.

The first clash between MV and Gilera, Hailwood and Minter, came at Imola. In his book Minter described the battle like this: 'As the 500 cc event was due to begin, the sun shone brightly and the scene was well set. The flag dropped and it was first blood to the MV, with Hailwood rushing into the lead and his stablemate Silvio Grassetti right behind him. Both John (Hartle) and myself on our Gileras were in the hunt after a pathetic start, and after the first lap had edged ahead of Grassetti and were chasing Mike. On the fifth lap he was still some 400 yards in front of me and was taking some catching. At the end of lap 10 of the twenty-five lap race I was resting on Mike's rear wheel and on lap 12 was able to move into the lead and once ahead concentrated on opening up the gap between us.

'John was also moving up strongly and he too rushed ahead of Mike, giving a first and second to Gilera. But I often wonder just how I managed to win this race. About four laps from the finish the machine developed gear-box trouble and every time I got revs on in fourth, it jumped out of gear.'

The Gilera challenge, which had started so dramatically, was sadly to fizzle out before the end of the season. First Minter had a serious crash at Brands, but made a remarkable personal recovery. Then Hartle crashed. In Ireland Minter complained that the Gilera was handling badly and this was followed soon afterwards by an argument with Duke. In the meantime, Hailwood was racing to the World Championship on the MV for the second year running. He was to gain it twice before Agostini took over.

During the 'sixties, admiration for the Japanese bikes and the MV was widespread in Britain, but there were secret longings for some sort of stake by the old country in this exciting period of racing revival. Oh for the golden days of Norton, AJS and Matchless.

Then, early in 1966, news broke which set our hearts pounding. Geoff Duke, former Norton and Gilera team star and the man behind the Gilera come-back attempt three years earlier, was now involved in a new sensation, plans for the building of a Velocette-BRM World Championship machine financed by funds from the Manx lottery.

Barely had we time to recover from this thrilling news when Dr Josef Ehrlich, Austrian born and the acknowledged authority behind the de Havilland EMC which for some five years from 1960 entered most of the 125 cc classic events and did well against the Japanese machines, announced that he had plans for a revolutionary 180 mph 500 cc British two-stroke multi. It was to be a private venture with anticipated support from British component manufacturers.

This was staggering news. Here was the possibility of *two* world beaters from Britain. Back went our thoughts to the dashing, daring 'thirties when British bikes were the best and the fastest in the world.

Dr Ehrlich reported that the engine design had been completed and small factory premises in Hertfordshire acquired in readiness for the building of the British World Beater.

Hell raisers everywhere were ravenous for more news of the projects. But as appetites increased, hard news and optimism grew thinner, There would be no British World Beater in 1966. That quickly became obvious. Prospects looked bleak as it became known that the Velocette-BRM project was struggling. Unless Sir Alfred Owen came to the rescue there appeared little hope of the new 'dream machine' ever being produced.

Dr Ehrlich's once proud vision foundered also.

The trouble with the British world beater projects in the 'sixties was that logic and emotion were at loggerheads – and logic came out on top. Murray Walker, BBC motor sport correspondent who has spent much of his life watching and reporting motor cycle racing, revealed the problem in very clear terms when asked to comment at the time. He said: 'Britain *could* produce a world beater, but whether she will is a different matter. In terms of engineering brilliance Britain is second to no nation and a country that can produce the BRM, the Lotus, the BMC Mini and the magnificent range of Rolls-Royce and Coventry-Climax engines could easily produce a racing motor cycle to challenge and, in my view, eventually beat, the Japanese and Italians.

'For us to do so, two other vital ingredients are needed: money and will-power. They come from either a giant concern like Honda, which needs racing success to help build its name and reputation, or a passionately enthusiastic tycoon like Count Agusta, the driving force behind MV, or the late Tony Vandervell, who put Britain back at the top of car racing with the Vanwall.'

At the time neither of the two big motor cycle manufacturers in Britain, BSA/Triumph and Norton-Villiers, seemed able to invest heavily enough in an attempt to make a name for themselves or for Britain in World Championship road racing, and once more we were left to relive former glories in memories of the past.

Though the 'sixties brought big bike clashes between Honda and MV, Phil Read on the Yamaha established a world reputation for himself and the Japanese factory in the less powerful classes. He took the 250 cc World Title in 1964, repeated his success in 1965 and 1968 and, amid the bitter feud with Bill Ivy, also secured the 125 cc World Title that same year.

Hailwood, Agostini, Ivy, Redman and Read . . . this was the circus which dominated top international racing in the 'sixties. Read wrestled for the headlines and found his fair share. As the decade began to run out he supported the Weslake project which again aimed to put a British racer back on top. He offered his services free for testing and racing the machine.

Less than a year later it was all off. Phil quit the Weslake project after riding the new racer on its only appearance, at

the North-West 200 in Ireland, when it failed to complete a lap
because of lubrication problems. There was no Weslake at the
TT, nor did it appear at events in which it had been entered
with Phil as rider. Faced with tempting cash offers for the 1970
season, Phil pulled out of the project and decided to concentrate again on full-time racing.

In the streaking world of outright speed on two wheels, the
'sixties turned up plenty of excitement. For six years nobody
had been able officially to advance W. Herz's record of 210
mph set up in 1956 on the 499 cc NSU. Along came American
Bill Johnson in 1962. He took his special 649 cc Triumph to
Bonneville Salt Flats, and at an official average of 224.5 mph
conclusively outstripped Herz.

Johnson, for four years, was the fastest man on two wheels,
but in 1966 speed-king Bob Leppan presented himself at
Bonneville in a sophisticated, glass-fibre, super-streamlined
projectile powered by two 650 cc Triumph engines, and flashed
over the salt flats at 247.67 mph, his average coming out at
245.67 mph.

Because the run was made under American motor cycle
Association auspices, an organisation which is not recognised
by the Federation Internationale Motorcycliste (FIM) in Europe,
Leppan's feat was not an official World Record, though to a
man we marvelled at the incredible performance. For Bob it
was the exhilarating accomplishment of twelve years' hard
struggle to become the world's fastest motor cycle rider, though
his remarkable machine showed little resemblance to the traditional bike. Low, long and cigar-shaped, it looked more like the
latest creation to traverse the vastness of outer space.

The 'sixties bred a new breed of motor cycle racer – a speed
ace who knew his own worth and spoke his own mind. Official
bodies and authorities had a tough time containing these outspoken aces who criticised race organisation, complained about
start money, rebelled against what they considered were petty
restrictions and hidebound rules. The TT, with it's appalling
low cash rewards was repeatedly condemned, but most riders
continued to race there. Temperaments were never so much in
evidence.

Top riders were celebrities whose attendance at a meeting
could put 10,000 on the gate. They were heroes, besieged by

autograph hunters whenever they appeared. They were part of the boom which the Beatles had brought to Britain. Gone for ever was the grubby image of the motor cycle racer with oily fingernails and B.O. They were the glamour boys of the Grands Prix. For the select few who raced with the backing of a works contract, the rewards were enormous.

Not surprisingly, there was a cut-and-thrust about international racing in the 'sixties which had not been experienced before. With the Japanese factories fully committed to an ambitious racing programme, there were rich rewards to be had by the riders who could get themselves noticed. Winning was never before so vital. With four and five figure contracts being held out by the Japanese, some riders weren't too fussy about cutting in on the corners, leaning, and elbowing their way to the front. Motor cycle racing became of age and grew into a glittering, glistening spectacle.

Out of sight, yet dominating the scene through their vision, passion and patriotism, were two men – Count Agusta of Italy and Soichiro Honda of Japan. They seldom attended race meetings, yet theirs was the ultimate power behind most of racing's activity, excitement and drama. Both quickly became legends in their own time.

Domenico Agusta inherited his father's aircraft business in 1927, but after the Second World War he founded MV Agusta in order to build motor cyles. Racers were introduced in 1950 and a four cylinder 500 which was to gain lasting fame came a little later. John Surtees joined the Italian firm in 1956 and that same year gained the 500 cc World Championship for MV, breaking the four year domination of this class by Gilera. MV failed to repeat their success in 1957 when Gilera, through Libero Liberati, took the title, but in 1958, with John Surtees in full cry and Gilera retired from racing, MV regained the title.

So began the astounding MV monopoly which stretched without interruption through the remainder of the 'fifties and the whole of the 'sixties. Through their deeds astride the powerful MVs, John Surtees, Gary Hocking, Mike Hailwood and Giacomo Agostini gained immortality in the folklore of motor cycle racing.

The Count's unswerving commitment to world supremacy

was hardly impeded, as little opposition remained in the big bike field once Gilera and Guzzi had quit, though Honda mounted a fierce campaign later in the 'sixties. Yet the ultimate objective was not achieved without the supreme sacrifice. Les Graham, who joined the Italian company in 1952 and rode with destinction that same year to capture one or two Grands Prix, put MV in an enviable position for an assault on the title the following year; but he was killed in the Senior TT while battling for the lead.

This tragic race was won by Rhodesian Ray Amm, a slim, religious rider with a startlingly hairy technique, who also took the Junior TT title that same year. But Ray too, was to die while riding an MV. It was at Imola on Easter Monday, 1955. Amm had turned his back more than once on offers from the Count, preferring to ride Norton. MV were determined and persistent. Finally he agreed to ride for the Italian factory. Tragically, in his very first race on the MV he lost control on a bend, was hurled off the machine, slid down a bank and struck his head on a partially hidden concrete post. He died shortly afterwards.

By 1961 Count Agusta could see his world crumbling. He lost control of the 125 cc and 250 cc classes as the Japanese attack moved into its stride. A year later he saw the 350 cc class disappear to Honda. The prospects looked bleak for the Count, but his determination to hang on to the 500 cc class was unwavering, and outstandingly successful. And miraculously, with a new three-cylinder racer, he almost recaptured the 350 cc crown in 1965 through Agostini.

Autocrat, patriot, determined to the point of near obsession, Count Agusta was also a shrewd businessman. At the time of his death in 1971 his industrial empire employed some 5,000 people, was the second largest manufacturer of helicopters in the world, and had deeply etched a name for itself in the history of motor cycle racing. His capacity for survival and his will to win were powerful characteristics. They brought him some 30 victories in the TT races and more than 60 individual and manufacturers world titles.

For Count Agusta, motor cycle racing was little more than a hobby. For Soichiro Honda motor cycle racing from the start was a business. There the dissimilarity ended. Both had unshakeable resolve, dynamism and courage to be internationally successful. Honda symbolised the post-war miracle of the Japanese. A professional motor engineer, he began his astonishing build-up of the Honda empire by using reconditioned army surplus power units. Working in the firm's research establishment his was the brain and the driving force behind the development of faster running units with greater reliability. He built up the biggest motor cycle business ever known and his racing machines conquered the world.

The string of famous riders who turned out for Honda reads like a Who's Who of motor cycle racing. Hailwood was the most dynamic, but there was also Jim Redman, Luigi Taveri, Ralph Bryans, Bill Ivy, Mike Duff, Phil Read, Frank Perris, Stuart Graham, Paddy Driver, Hugh Anderson, Hans-Georg Anscheidt, Tom Phillis, and many many more.

In the 'sixties more money than ever before was invested in racing. It was the golden era. Responsible for it, more than any other single item, was the determination of the Japanese to gain world supremacy. Ex-Honda works mechanic Nobby Clark once estimated it cost Honda around £20,000 to develop the 50-twin and that each bike put an additional £2,000 to £5,000 on the bill. Development of the 250-six and the 500-four, and putting them on the race track, would cost proportionately more. Riders were allowed to name their own price... and the Japanese were so passionately committed to ultimate success that they paid up... with little complaint.

The Honda and Yamaha circuses were lavish, incorporating large transports, superb back-up equipment and spares, and a small army of mechanics and managers. At one time Honda were reputed to have 11 mechanics on their books, Yamaha had six and Suzuki four... all at a weekly wage of around £50. To this was added the considerable cost of hotels and travel around the world for riders, mechanics, staff and bikes. The total cost of the massive Japanese bid for world motor cycle racing supremacy was said to have run into millions.

Never had the spending been so lavish, the commitment so total. The result was perhaps, as Nobby Clark believes, a motor cycle the like of which had not been seen before. The Honda-4 should have been Honda's final scaling of the Everest of motor cycle racing. Yet the immense power which was intended to give it world domination was responsible for its failure. It was this power, in Nobby Clark's view, which gave the machine such appalling handling characteristics.

In 1969 Nobby Clark said he believed that Honda would return to racing, perhaps in 1971. By that time, however, the European controlled FIM had changed the formula, thus preventing the Japanese works bikes as we knew them from competing. But he said: 'When the Japanese return to racing it will be on their own terms. Gone for ever are the days of multi-thousand pound race contracts, except perhaps for one or two riders – or at the most one per factory.'

So it seems the golden age of motor cycle racing will never return. The big spend is over. Perhaps too the hope of a full scale, works supported Japanese revival is little more than a pipe dream. We had the same high hopes for the return of Guzzi and Gilera a decade before.

But the memories of these glorious 'sixties remain

# 2
# Tearaway Bill - Racing's Rebel

Bill Ivy was a flamboyant character and an exciting motor cycle racer. His abandoned, fearless style won him a multitude of fans and took him to the brink of disaster more than once. When the end came the tragic news left me limp and drained.

I was stretched out on my garden lounger, comfortably dozing, when my elder daughter, Sarah, rushed out of the house: 'Bill Ivy's dead,' she shouted. 'They've just said so on the radio.'

The crushing brutality of the news was in total contrast to the safety and solitude of the garden around me. I was convinced there must be some mistake.

Tragically there was, of course, no mistake. Bill Ivy, road racing's mighty little atom, *was* dead, killed in practice at Sachsenring. For some sad moments I lost myself in a flashback of memories of the diminutive Kent boy who had a giant's courage and became a world champion.

I remembered having lunch with him in his favourite West End Restaurant, La Potette, just behind Harrods. The sleek Ferrari was parked outside and there was a bright and attractive dolly-girl snuggled by his side. I wanted him to do his autobiography and offered help with the writing. He was interested until he heard the sum of money a publisher had offered for his story. At the time he was under contract to Yamaha and he told me politely, but very directly, that it just wasn't worth his while to spend time on a book for the sum the publisher was offering.

I tried a different tactic. Bill had a keen appreciation of his own talents, so perhaps I could appeal to his ego. Wouldn't he like his own story written down in book form with his name prominently displayed on the front cover? Think of the prestige,

28

the fan appeal it would bring, I reasoned, with personal appearances at book shops and autograph sessions at circuits round the world. It would be a permanent record of his contribution to motor cycle racing. For a moment I thought I had him convinced, but if Bill had a fine regard for his own abilities he was even more acutely sensitive to the money he reckoned his reputation and standing ought to bring him. Finally we abandoned the idea.

I remembered the friendly telephone conversations I enjoyed with Bill's mother, Mrs Nell Ivy, who genuinely wanted to help me. I know she wanted Bill's contribution to the race game to go down in print, but even a mother's influence was insufficient for Bill where money was concerned. He thought he was worth more than my publisher was prepared to advance and that was all there was to it.

I remembered the hairiness of some of Bill's early rides as a private racer and of the prediction of that wily old fox, Derek Minter, who told me a long time ago that Bill would come to grief on the track.

But I remembered, most of all, the outstanding contribution that Bill had made to motor cycle racing in so short a time, how he had epitomised the newly emerging image of the motor cycle racing super-star with a works contract and a jet-set life, and how, for all his size (just 5 ft. 3 in.) there had been no more colourful and exciting personality than his during the whole of the Swinging 'Sixties.

Let us not be over reverential to his memory. Bill wouldn't thank us for it. He was no angel and well he knew it. Often rude, frequently over-aggressive to authority and discipline, and at times impossibly self centred for many would-be fans, his career was turbulent and often explosive. Yet behind the arrogance was an impish cheek which most of us found irresistible. In spite of his vast earnings, large cars, hanger-on girl friends and almost constant world travel, he was at heart naïve. Seldom was he out of the headlines. He made an impact on the race game that has not been equalled since his passing.

The climax of Ivy's phenomenal career was undoubtedly the duels he fought with Yamaha team-mate Phil Read in 1968. It started as friendly rivalry, but developed into a bitter situation when Phil Read refused to hold back to allow Bill, who was occupying a better position, to take the championship. Read continued racing to win. A bitter feud developed between the team-mates and in September, after Read had crossed the line to win the 250 cc race in the Italian Grand Prix, Bill lodged an on-the-spot protest alleging that Read's front number plate did not conform to FIM specifications and that his chain was not of the make he was under contract to use.

It was a maddened reaction, unworthy of a rider of Bill Ivy's talent, but it displayed his absolute frustration and anger at a situation he didn't really know how to handle. Bill Ivy loved to be liked and admired for his swash-buckling performances on the circuits, and in the conflict with Read he could see his success in danger of being snatched from him.

Bill's protest was rejected. Read, handling the situation more coolly, commented 'I can't imagine making such an obviously transparent protest,' to which an even more enraged Ivy retorted: 'If people say it's bad sportsmanship, it's all right with me. I'm a bad sportsman. Being a good one didn't do me any good.' Later Ivy said: 'I had nothing to lose. Before the race Read said if I won he would protest that I was under the FIM minimum weight of 9 stone 6 lb."

The once harmonic relationship was now well and truly washing its dirty linen in public and was to end (see chapter 15) in a peeved and disillusioned Bill Ivy quitting the race game in a flurry of damning criticism of the 'bickering and back-biting'.

'I am too sensitive to stand it,' he announced.

Bill had missed the world title. That was hard for him to take. Even harder was Yamaha's apparent reaction, for on his return from Monza it was reported that Read received a cable of congratulation from the Japanese factory. It was all too much for Bill to accept.

How different it all had been nine years earlier when a young, tentative Bill Ivy had started racing a 50 cc Itom, sponsored by Chisholms of Maidstone, the motor cycle dealers. He won his very first race and a phenomenal career was born. Bill's natural talent was excitingly displayed at the final meeting at Brands Hatch in that same year, 1959, when he captured the lap record for the short circuit.

Like most 'overnight successes' Bill Ivy had his share of

disappointments, setbacks and frustrations. 1960 was a black year. He crashed heavily while riding a Triumph Thunderbird and hit a telegraph pole. He smashed his pelvis and both legs, the left leg in five places. That leg was in plaster for nearly six months and he spent a month in hospital. Yet six weeks after the plaster came off he was back on a competition bike winning his first race of the 1961 season.

And when he first entered the TT, in 1962, he retired on the first lap.

He raced for Geoff Monty before moving on in 1965 to Tom Kirby, for whom he rode AJS and Matchless machines. Said Geoff of him: 'Bill was a quick learner and very brave. He had a natural feel for an engine and could get the most out of it. He could lift a big bike from the ground without trying.'

With Kirby he was an outstanding success, winning the first 500 cc races he entered for his new sponsor, and crowning a superlative season with the British Championship title. It was the start of big things.

After riding a spectacular race at Brands Hatch on a factory 250 cc Yamaha, he was offered 125 cc and 250 cc machines by the renowned Japanese factory. His big chance came in the Japanese Grand Prix. Ivy finished fourth in the 125 cc event and third on a 250 cc machine. Yamaha, hungry for international success, were impressed. They saw Ivy's potential and invited him to sign a works contract. Bill's short life as a superstar had begun.

From the time young Bill Ivy left school to go into the AMC competitions department at Woolwich and then to work for Chisholms of Maidstone, his aim had been a professional motor cycle racing career. He realised that ambition in 1965 and from then on his confidence, stature and reputation grew rapidly. His appetite for racing was insatiable. He celebrated a successful season by getting engaged to Ann Happe – and buying a British racing green 'E' Type Jaguar. The Ivy flair was already beginning to show.

Later the Jag made way for a silver Ferrari and a scarlet Chevrolet Stingray. His engagement to Ann Happe was broken off. Attractive Penny Allen became his girl friend – but Bill never did marry and said more than once that marriage and motor cycling didn't mix. Penny, a photographic model in

London, was Bill's girl friend at the time of his death. They weren't officially engaged – 'we had an understanding and didn't consider an official engagement necessary,' said Penny. Two-and-a-half years after Bill died Penny re-lived for me the past which at the time was very much part of her future: 'I was not part of the motor cycle set really. I got to know Bill through Mike (Hailwood). I'd known Bill for four years and we were going to be married. His flamboyance was a front. He was really rather shy. He was a colourful character with a good personality: a lovely person, sweet and never nasty to anyone.'

He raced often and won a lot. But winning, or not winning, Ivy as a Yamaha professional was seldom out of the headlines. He wallowed in the glory and glamour of his new found status as a world racing star. It was one sure way little Bill could be a giant. He was a consistent rebel. He relished the reputation. Constantly he made news.

At Rimini he was involved in a scuffle with a spectator. The series of incidents that led up to the scuffle, which resulted in police intervention, had started a week before when Bill, while racing in the West German Grand Prix, crashed in the 125 race. Delayed shock set in and he was afterwards taken to hospital, but Bill defied the German doctors' orders to stay in hospital for a few days. Instead he travelled to Rimini for the following Sunday's racing. As he was besieged by autograph hunters, a girl fan was said to have been pushed or punched in the crush. Her boyfriend, it was alleged, began to kick the side of Ivy's car. Bill reacted sharply and the fight which ensued was broken up by an Italian journalist and photographer.

Back home we read that he had bought Mike Hailwood's flat at Heston near London Airport. His instant friendship with Hailwood angered many of his critics.

They felt it all just a little too convenient. Hailwood was the millionaire's son, the glamour boy of motor cycle racing. Stick close to him and some of the gloss is bound to rub off. That is what Bill's critics alleged. But I personally doubt that this was true. Bill's mother, Nell Ivy, also insists that this was not the case. 'Bill was genuinely fond of Mike. There is no doubt about that,' she said. 'In fact it was Mike's suggestion that Bill should take over the flat. Flats were difficult and expensive and Mike didn't really want two flats.' And his sister, Mrs Suzette Swift, also totally rejects the possibility. 'Bill crawl round Mike? – those who say so must be joking. Mike can spot a crawler a mile off.' It is certainly true that Ivy stimulated criticism among some fans and riders for no other reason that he was too successful for them too early in his career.

At the Belgian Grand Prix Bill Ivy was manhandled by two Belgian policemen. On the Isle of Man he made headlines yet again when he crashed his £5,000, 150 mph Ferrari GT car. He later reported that the repair bill was over £1,000! The sequel to the crash was a £12 fine, after he pleaded guilty to driving the car in 'a manner dangerous to the public'. His licence was endorsed and the police witness said that he thought that the car, with Mike Hailwood and two women as passengers, was travelling at 50 mph when it crashed into a wall. Ivy, he said, had stated that the rear tyre had punctured. And racing at Brands Hatch he crashed at 120 mph during practice – but was unhurt.

In Italy, racing at Riccione, he braked late in a furious duel with Hans-Georg Anscheidt riding a Suzuki and shot up a slip road. He was held by Italian police, who feared a collision if he rode back on to the circuit, but he argued his way back into the race – to win and also to smash the 125 cc lap record.

At the Belgian Grand Prix Bill was roughly pushed aside by two local policemen when he tried to enter the paddock before practice was due to start. Ivy, who later admitted he didn't have a pass but claimed that he was told he didn't need one for practice, said he was knocked down and kicked before being carried off to a police van. Said Bill: 'I tried to explain, but the coppers started pushing and shoving.' John Robinson, World Champion sidecar passenger, saw the incident, went for help, and Ivy was released.

At Cadwell Park Bill was stung by a wasp while racing... but still managed to finish the day with a lap record, an outright win and two second places to his credit!

On the track Bill Ivy was fearless and he rode many spectacular races. 'He was a bit of a dasher,' as Derek Minter called him, but he had outstanding courage.

Off the track his brash showmanship won him an international reputation in a couple of years. He talked openly, as no other racing star had ever done, about booze and birds, and very quickly Bill Ivy became the front-runner, both on a race machine and in selling his own image as something of a playboy. In an article in *Motor Cycle News* he said 'After the race in Spain we had a bit of a booze-up. A few drinks help you to relax, but I don't touch the stuff during practice or before the race' . . . 'I still go out with the dollies and when I have a ball I really have a ball, but racing comes first' . . . 'After I fell off at Brands I got well slewed because I was so happy that I could crash at 120 mph and still be healthy enough to go out in the evening' . . . 'My car is an American Stingray which I bought last year from Luigi Taveri. It is a great crumpet-wagon and I like ginormous engines. I think I will have another one this year, but with a seven litre motor.'

It all made great material for the press, but was it the real Ivy talking . . . or the man he was pretending to be?

He was the first rider to sport a Beatle hairdo, which put him into trouble with the Germans, who hated it. He relished his notoriety. To his public he was tough, unyielding, boastful and gloriously outrageous. His racing was always exciting and displayed that touch of arrogance. Ivy undeniably had star quality. He relished the thrills of racing, the off track fame, the jet-set travel from one famous circuit to another, the lucrative works contract, the expensive cars, the girls in a score of countries who flocked to see him and tried to share his bed. Off track Bill Ivy's firebrand personality resulted in regular skirmishes. Racing, he projected a dashing professionalism, thrilling crowds with many inspired performances.

He was a world champion only once but his race distinctions were many. Back in April, 1966, he achieved an early objective by taking the King of Brands title away from Derek Minter. Derek had trouble with his Seeley Matchless, but Bill bettered a Dave Degens in magnificent form and a powerful 350 Honda-mounted Mike Hailwood to be acclaimed the conqueror before a 35,000 crowd.

Two days later he secured his first classic win, going ahead of such world class opposition as Taveri and Bryans on Hondas and Phil Read on a Yamaha, to take the 125 cc event in Spain. Ivy's domination was exceptional. The powerful five-cylinder Hondas were well outpaced by the water-cooled twin ridden by Bill.

The same month, at Clermont-Ferrand, Ivy won the 250 cc event at the French Grand Prix. Early laps produced an exciting battle between the 'works' trio of Ivy and Read on Yamahas and Hailwood on the Honda 'six, Then Mike began to pull away. Twelve laps gone, four to go, and Mike, now in a seemingly invincible position, 'lost' gears on a corner and lost time while things were put right. Read, his machine also in trouble, went through just as Mike started up again, but Bill Ivy was very close behind. With both Hailwood and Read struggling against missed gears, a cheeky Bill nipped through and pulled away to win.

Ivy, 1968, is remembered for his first Italian 125 cc and 250 cc double victory, and his history-making performances at the Isle of Man when he claimed a new Mountain Circuit lap record of 105.51 mph, topping Mike Hailwood's previous 250 cc record by more than 12 secs. Bill, in superlative form, also became the first man to lap the course at over 100 mph on a 125 cc bike. His speed, during practice, was 100.14 mph. Bill's 250 cc victory was won in spite of a right foot injured when he got it caught negotiating the twisty circuit through Milntown. He twisted his ankle, cut his toes and tore his boot ... but Bill, later being helped to the winner's rostrum, forgot about his discomforts in the excitement of victory. A watching Agostini paid warm tribute to Bill's performance: 'His standing start lap was as fast as I have done in practice on a 350 MV from a *flying start*, and I thought that I was going very quickly.'

A month later Bill retired battered and shaken when the treacherous surface of the Brno circuit in Czechoslovakia took his machine from under him. Just when he was struggling to overcome a depressing run of defeats and crashes, he scored a magnificent success at the Ulster Grand Prix, winning both the 125 cc and 250 cc events. He established a new speed record in the former and raced the fastest lap in the latter.

Two months later came the dramatic public row with Read and the once-glittering race game had gone bad on him. Ironically perhaps the milk had begun to turn sour at the end of December 1967 when the rumours were strong that Ivy and not his team-mate Phil Read would be first string for Yamaha the following season. Until this point the partnership of Read and Ivy had seemed harmonious and the two had done well for Yamaha. There had seldom been tantrums and few star riders had ridden better together. But perhaps Read didn't like the possibility of Ivy taking over. In 1968 Yamaha fiercely pursued both the 125 cc and 250 cc world titles. With typical Japanese commitment they were determined to take the honours. They didn't care who rode the winning bikes, Ivy or Read, so long as the titles were won.

The relationship between the two riders steadily worsened as tensions grew and came to a peak in an outright feud. Bill was out-manoeuvred and out-scored. Read, in the wider sphere of human experience, left Bill well behind. Ivy seemed to be psychologically battered and bruised. In October that year he quit the race game, complaining: 'I now realise that I was never happier than when I was working as a mechanic when I started racing.'

Suddenly the flamboyance and the arrogance was no more. He went on: 'The only thing I am thankful for is that I am alive. There have been times when I thought racing would leave me before I left racing. I have ceased to be interested and never want to race again.'

No matter how resolutely the assertion is made, there is something about the race game which makes former stars return. The very next season the offer of a contract to ride 350 cc Jawa 4s brought Bill Ivy back to the race track. Bill, in fact, had done all the running. After vehemently announcing his disgust with, and retirement from, racing at the end of the 1968 season, he was, by January the very next year, making strong efforts to secure a ride for the approaching season. Yamaha, meantime, had retired from racing and Bill wrote first to Jawa in Czechoslovakia and then to Benelli, offering his services. Benelli turned him down, but he was later invited to Prague for talks with Jawa and a contract was signed.

With his wide experience of racing multi-cylinder two-strokes with Yamaha, Bill was the right man for the Jawa job. They knew it and so did he. The Ivy magic, dangerously close to being lost for the 1969 season, was now assured. Fans were delighted. He didn't disappoint them. In West Germany and Holland he notched brilliant second places. Bill was back with all the old dash and daring.

Then came the disaster to end it all. At 26 years old,

practising for the East German Grand Prix, he crashed as he raced towards Hohensteim Ernstthal. A piston on his 4-cylinder 350 cc Jawa 2-stroke seized and locked the rear wheel. The machine skidded across the road. Bill's helmet came off and he received severe head injuries when he struck the low wall of a garden fence. Although he was rushed to hospital and put in an oxygen tent, Bill Ivy's life was at an end.

Everything Ivy did and said, was potential drama, often of his own making, but not always. When he was called to prove his worth for Yamaha, with an almost certain works contract should they be impressed, the circumstances were so exciting as to be almost make-believe. Racing a car at Brands, he was flagged down and told that Phil Read was on the telephone from Japan. Phil told Bill that Mike Duff had been injured in practice and Yamaha wanted Bill as a replacement rider for the Japanese Grand Prix. He had been out of the country only once before. Now he was off half way across the world to Japan. He caught a plane the very next day.

Bill impressed Yamaha and before leaving Japan signed a contract to race for them in the 1966 World Championship events.

It was Phil Read, later to squabble with Bill when personal honour was at stake, who first introduced him to Yamaha. At Read's invitation Ivy rode Yamaha's new 250 cc and 125 cc twins at Silverstone and in bad conditions did well. As a result Bill was asked to race for them on the Isle of Man and at the Dutch TT. Then came Duff's timely, for Bill, spill in Japan and after that he was firmly in the Yamaha saddle.

When Bill died much of the fire of motor cycle racing in the 'sixties was gone. But now, in the 'seventies, the Ivy name remains in racing to remind us of an incredible, if brief, period of motor cycle history. Yamaha, in recognition of the achievements Bill had secured in their name, presented Bill's mother with the 350 cc TR3 used by Bill only once and Mrs Ivy, helped considerably by Romford dealer-entrant Tom Kirby, decided to sponsor a rider instead of selling the bike to raise money. She chose Rex Butcher, who first raced the 'Ivy-Yamaha', as the bike was re-christened. Mrs Ivy kept her son's memory alive by having an impressive trophy made incorporating a solid silver crash helmet and a large ivy leaf engraved on the front, to be won by the successful rider in a series of Bill Ivy Challenge Races.

In spite of his public image Bill was basically an orderly and meticulous person, particularly towards the end. Mrs Ivy told me: 'When we had to go through his things all his papers were properly kept even down to a list of people who owed him money. We had no trouble at all because everything was in order'.

It was difficult for all but his closest friends to pierce the public crust that was Bill Ivy to find out what he was really like. His character was far more complicated than the side he liked to present to his public. His generosity was not generally known, but his friends will tell you how he would give generously in peculiar ways, not always financial. For someone in real need he would do a lot, even if he didn't really know the person concerned, but this was a private side of little Bill that he insisted on keeping private.

One example of his generosity concerned an ex-girl friend involved in a serious car crash. Bill made a point of visiting her in hospital, spent about half an hour chatting with her, came home and told his family how she was getting along, and then went back to London. So far as his family knew, that was the end of it, but one day some months later, Bill's sister met the girl and the story came out. Bill had quietly made arrangements for the girl to be transferred to a private room at his expense and had telephoned her every day to cheer her up.

I talked to his sister Mrs Suzette Swift about Bill's girl friends. 'Yes ... Bill loved them, married ones and single ones; they were all fun to be with. Bill loved to be seen around with a beauty, but a pretty girl was a prop to him. His associations were all out in the open. He didn't hide them away in hotel bedrooms. If he had a girl, everyone knew about it. He loved the pop image it gave him, but girls were never just a sex object to him.'

His friends are agreed that for quite a while before his death, Bill was devoted to Penny Allen and would do nothing to offend her.

The book I wanted Bill to write was never started in the form we talked about. Mrs Ivy feels sure that was because Bill was determined to write it himself, in his own way and without help. But after Bill's death Alan Peck's excellent biography of a young man who rapidly became the most dynamic star of the 'sixties is certainly just tribute for a motor cycle racer who made the supreme sacrifice for the game. It also revealed once more the complex personality of Bill and underlined yet again his astonishing capacity for creating interest, speculation, controversy and impact in a sport, which, for all the excitement of the 'sixties, badly needed it. Alan reported how in the weeks leading up to the fatal accident Ivy was threatened with a growing fear of impending disaster and even the circumstances of his final crash were not totally clear. That his Jawa seized there is little doubt, but an eye witness reported that he took his left hand off the handlebar to adjust the position of his helmet or goggles at the precise time his engine seized. As Peck described it: 'If he had his left hand off the bars he would never have reached the clutch in time to release the drive to the back wheel.

'During the crash Ivy's helmet came off but why it should have done remains a mystery. One theory is that he had not fastened the helmet strap properly, and was in the act of doing so when the Jawa seized.' He made headlines to the end.

When Bill Ivy died Tom Kirby, his early sponsor and friend, said: 'Bill was 10 feet tall by my reckoning. He was one of the world's greatest. Sensitive about his small stature he rebelled against authority and could not stand anything phony. Bill raced as he lived – fast and spectacularly. We have lost a great champion.'

We also lost a special kind of hell raiser, who perhaps more than any other champion, typified a swinging Britain with changing ideas for the world.

# 3

# Speeding for the Gold

The prospect of getting rich quick has driven many a hell raiser on to the race circuits of the world. With John Cooper it was different. He wasn't prepared to travel extensively abroad. Or he didn't get the opportunity at the right time. Yet in Britain John always had the happy knack of winning the big one; the one which paid the most money. And when he did eventually contest America's famous Ontario event, he came back richer by £6,000.

But that's John Cooper all over. Often under-estimated, generally eclipsed in the 'sixties by the more glamorous bachelor-gay Grand Prix racers, he always had much more skill, cunning, technique, dash and daring than his earlier reputation suggested. He raced first in 1954 when he was sixteen. Seventeen years later Cooper was still around, not just making up the numbers, but capturing the headlines with his big-race victories and top-money prizes.

Incredibly, 1971 was by far John Cooper's most outstanding season. Incredibly, because by then he was 34 years old and not readily recognised as a new contender for the premier place in British racing. He scored outstanding victories at Mallory Park and Brands Hatch, outshining even world champion Agostini. Then he went to America. He won the Champion Spark Plug Classic in California and came back a hero.

From three races John netted almost £9,000. He was raved about in the United States. In Britain he was the new idol, though he had been around for years and years.

Cooper had been in the race game so long we had almost forgotten he was there. At least twice he said he would retire, then didn't. In spite of the mooneyes painted on his helmet and which picked him out from the crowd, Cooper had never rated too strongly in public relations terms. The mooneyes certainly helped. They were a good idea. He'd previously had a 'Jiminy Cricket' on his helmet. Then he spotted some 'mooneyes' in a shop and as he had just had his helmet sprayed red, he thought the eyes would stand out. They constituted a new idea at the time, but in spite of this, in the dazzling days of the 'sixties he was not spectacular as a racing celebrity, nor particularly exciting. His outstanding successes at Mallory Park, and in particular in the Race of the Year, didn't bring him due credit. We all too readily put it down to Mallory being John's home circuit. He knew it better than anyone else. He naturally had the edge on the other boys there.

Exactly like others, he crashed, had mechanical failures, went off form, said too much for his own good, and won races in impressive style. Yet somehow, Cooper could never quite generate super-star acceptance. He suffered, as Minter did, from being a home-based rider. He had no role to play in the sensations of the 'sixties. But when the Grand Prix circus had ended, when the Japanese had long since left the arena, John Cooper was still there: riding his best races; enjoying belated adulation; cornering the market in big-money wins.

In 1969 he almost quit. A bad fall at Cadwell Park chipped at his confidence and at 32 the temptation to call it a day and concentrate on developing his garage business was great. A new, exciting bike called the Yamsel kept him racing.

Although John had always admired the engines of the Yamahas which speedway star Barry Briggs had got for him from America, he acknowledged the bike's difficult handling. On the other hand his own AJS 7R handled beautifully, but the machine was too slow against more up-to-date machinery. The object of the new Yamsel was to fuse the best characteristics of the two machines; and John found the possibilities in such a development too exciting to resist.

The Yamsel, with a 350 cc TA2 Yamaha engine in a modified Seeley frame, gave John the impetus he needed. Out of 23 races he won eighteen and crossed the line first in Mallory's lucrative Race of the Year. Who could deny that Cooper was now the supreme exponent of short circuit racing in Britain? In the Race of the Year, John not only outpaced and outstayed some of the best British competition including Phil Read, Paul

Smart and Peter Williams, but he also stayed ahead of American ace Gary Nixon on the latter's first race visit to Britain.

John didn't have an easy ride. To be fair, some of his toughest opposition eliminated itself. Percy Tait, Ray Pickrell, Ron Chandler and Dave Croxford all retired. Paul Smart was left on the line. So were Kel Carruthers and Steve Spencer. French-Canadian ace Yvon-du-Hamel suffered brake trouble. But Cooper won, and it is wins that count in races where you can pick up more than £1,000 in prize money.

Cooper enjoys uncanny success and popularity at Mallory. He knows every bump and crack. Nobody rushes into bends with more ease and confidence. Already winner of the Race of the Year three times, twice in successive years, his first victory was in 1965. With the methodical progression typical of Cooper, he had been slowly working up to it with a third in 1963 and a second in 1964. Were his fans hoping for too much in looking for the big one to come John's way in 1965?

Opposition talent was lavish: Mike Hailwood, Phil Read, Bill Ivy, Dave Degens, Paddy Driver and others. Their machinery, certainly the MV and Yamaha of Hailwood and Read, was much more sophisticated and by reputation a good deal faster than John's Norton.

Early season events had not favoured the Derby rider. Twice his engines had blown up. Twice there had been expensive re-builds. Even then he was unable to squeeze that extra bit of pace out of them to cross the line first. He called in ace-tuner Ray Petty and a Cadwell Park £200 triumph was the result.

Had Cooper's luck begun to turn? It seemed so, that autumn day in 1965. He had raced well in earlier outings, collecting thirds in both the 500 cc and 350 cc events. Rain during the afternoon was to John's advantage. He knew Mallory better than anyone there. He knew too, that the opposition would have to treat the wet surface with caution. There was another shower as the riders formed up for the Race of the Year and John might well have smiled quietly to himself at this stage. Fate, at least, seemed favourable.

The bikes blasted away, but from the start it was Hailwood and Read shooting to the front with Paddy Driver well up on his Matchless. John, easily identified by the mooneyes on his

helmet and by his rather upright head position, was close at
hand and had forced through into the lead at the Esses. Cooper
recalls: 'I was up in front for a couple of laps, but then Phil
Read on the Yamaha passed me and held grimly to the lead
for the next three laps.'

At this point Phil had the Yamaha moving beautifully and
John's chances seemed to fade. Bill Ivy was dangerously close
to his shoulder and Paddy Driver was well in touch behind
Ivy. Read began to pull away. John didn't give up. He forced
the Norton ahead, squeezing every inch of speed from it. By
lap 19 he was visibly closing the gap and the crowd came to
life again. He pulled back a lot of ground on that 19th lap
and was in the race again with a real chance. Said John afterwards: 'Phil was having trouble with the Yamaha. I was feeling
pretty good with things on lap 20 when at Gerards Bend I
managed to take him, and then open the gap between us. With
four of the 40 laps still to go I was really flying and had
secured a substantial lead. Then, just when I thought I had the
race in the bag, disaster: my clutch failed.'

Cooper was forced to cut back his speed and on the remaining four crucial, agonising laps, had to make clutchless changes.
He crossed the line only seconds ahead of Read, with Ivy in
third position.

John Cooper won his first event way back in 1954 when he
raced a 197 James for the first time. This was six years before
he registered his first big-time win at Scarborough. He became
350 cc British Champion in 1964, 350 cc and 500 cc British
Champion two years later. He added the 250 cc British Championship in 1968.

There was nothing excitingly dynamic about his progress
or his riding. He was competent and composed, but he wasn't
cracking the whip like many of his fans hoped he might and
at times progress seemed hard to come by. As a person he was
popular and well liked. His successes gave him second place
in *Motor Cycle News* 'Man of the Year' poll in 1964, but he
slipped to third place a year later.

As the 'sixties advanced, John Cooper seemed to have been
around for a tediously long time. Newer riders climbed over
him to make their mark on the international scene. John
plodded on unexcitingly and, disappointingly for his fans,

seemed to be making heavy weather of some of the events. Cooper's chance of world fame had surely come and gone in a fleeting moment back in 1964. Along with other 'available' privateers he was asked by works chiefs if he could beat Hailwood. Remembers Cooper: 'I said that given the chance I would try. Others said they *could* – and that made the difference.'

But John has a big heart for motor cycle racing and in spite of disappointments, setbacks and a public which began to consider him beyond his prime in racing terms, he stayed close to the centre of things. Too close perhaps. He was too much of a regular at home circuits ever to be considered a super-star. It is difficult to secure top billing when one is always on show. More and more he was talked about reflectively: on a works bike Cooper *could* have become a world champion; if he *had* raced more earnestly abroad as well as at home and given less attention to his business he might have done better; if only he *had* done more to attract the factory bosses.

He was virtually written off as he ran out of form in 1968. He crashed in the Ulster Grand Prix and said he would retire, but he was back riding in 1969. He crashed again, this time at Cadwell Park, and once again said he had had enough.

John, it seems, was destined always to be the good trier, the hard done by, the obvious champion if only ...

He pleaded he could prove how good he was given equal machinery. Nobody gave him equal machinery. He'd longed for a works bike, but a regular works ride never came.

John had missed the boat and even the most passionately faithful of his fans could see little future for the likeable, bespectacled rider from Derby. Doubts, self-recriminations, bitter disappointments were driven deeper in 1969 as Cooper was battered into the ground by the cruelty of a season as desperately unsuccessful as anything he had previous experienced.

Then sensationally, miraculously, John hoisted himself up from the abyss of despair. Within two short years he brought the race game throbbing back to life with dramatic victories at home and abroad. He was the man of the moment, a world beater. He had a fine season in 1970. He did even better in 1971, with fifteen firsts, six seconds and ten thirds ... plus fourteen fastest laps including four lap records. He made a hat-

trick of his Race of the Year successes and won the Brands
Hatch Race of the South.

As so often before Cooper had seemed at the crossroads as
he approached that 1971 Race of the Year. He had won it the
previous year in a good season. He could now go forward or
slide back once again and, a symbolic pointer if nothing more,
seemed to be the big one at Mallory.

A tough battle was predicted because Agostini was to compete on his power-packed 500cc MV, Cooper on his 750 cc
BSA Rocket. Tension was high as world champion Agostini
flashed into the lead and for 22 laps the Italian was in front.
Cooper kept well in touch and the drama mounted as he was
seen to be inching forward, closing on Ago. At the Esses John
took his chance, outriding Agostini and moving into the lead.
The 50,000 crowd went wild as they saw their local hero stay
in front for the remaining eight laps. Not only had Cooper
accomplished the impossible, he had done it at a new record
of 91.50 mph average for the race.

John predicted success in this race. And afterwards he said
excitedly: 'If I could lead into Gerards on the last lap I knew
I could win, because I was much quicker out of Gerards than
he was. When I reached the hairpin and his shadow wasn't
there I knew I had won. It was the hardest and greatest race
I have ever ridden.'

Although Cooper won, he got paid only half what Agostini
was guaranteed merely to appear, and complained that he had
to argue for days to make sure he got even that amount.

It was a magnificent start to the new season for Cooper. The
season ended in no less dramatic style. As if to demonstrate
that his Mallory victory was no fluke, he again took command
and was too good for Agostini in the Race of the South at
Brands Hatch in October. Twice now, in three races, John had
been superior to the handsome Italian. Again at Brands, Cooper
had been really travelling, reducing the lap record there by
one fifth of a second. His new absolute record for the 2.65 mile
circuit was 91.03 mph, accomplished on a 750 BSA.

It was the manner of John's win that thrilled the fans. He
never looked like losing to Ago. He moved into the lead at the
bottom straight the second time round, after Agostini had catapulted to the front at the start, and rode convincingly.

Shortly after, Cooper was acclaimed 'Man of the Year' by readers of *Motor Cycle News* for the second year running, equalling John Surtees' record. But more than that, he had a record number of votes cast for him and won by a record margin from Phil Read.

The whole of the racing scene had burst to life again and the once unexciting John Cooper, of all people, was the man responsible. Reported *Motor Cycle News* of the Brands Hatch meeting: 'With a best lap that knocked one fifth of a second off Mike Hailwood's 297 cc Honda 6 record of 1968 and victories in the Race of the South and in the final round of the Superbike series, Cooper may also have booked himself a works BSA for the rich Ontario race in America on October 17.'

In the midst of his new-found success, John Cooper seemed to be the most unimpressed of anybody. 'I'm riding no better now than I was years ago. It's just that I've never had a works bike before, a really competitive machine.'

BSA/Triumph, thrilled by John's success in their colours, hurried through plans for him to contest the world's richest race in America. American race fans had not seen Cooper before. His local reputation at Mallory or even in Britain meant nothing to them. They gave him no chance against their own aces in the gruelling Ontario event. But at Daytona, a calm Cooper carried the flag in spectacular fashion.

Not only did he win America's longest road race, but he did it first time out. Suddenly big Coop was everybody's darling. Norton desperately wanted him and made tempting overtures. John had talks with BSA and after a month of bargaining decided to stay with the factory which had brought him his greatest triumphs.

His exceptional success in 1971 was shared with BSA/Triumph Development Engineer Doug Hele and together they were the subject of interesting speculation prior to the 1972 season. It was no secret that Norton Villiers, determined to capture a greater stake in the lucrative American market, were after a development engineer and when the job was officially advertised there was great speculation that Hele had been approached to fill the vacancy. An internal reshuffle at Triumph which might affect the position of Doug Hele in that organisation, made the situation all that more intriguing.

Cooper, in the meantime, had also been approached by Norton. He was undecided, but rumour and speculation were scotched early in January when Hele said he would remain with BSA/Triumph. A week later Cooper, too, announced that he would stay with BSA/Triumph.

Norton, after being close to pulling off a great scoop with the signing of both Doug Hele and John Cooper, had missed them both. Cooper remained with BSA/Triumph for no other reason, though a justified one, that he wanted to stay with Hele, in spite of a higher cash offer from Frank Perris to join the John Player backed Norton team. Cooper told me: 'When brainbox Hele turned down that Norton offer I knew I would too.'

Lack of works bikes in the 'sixties denied John his chance of international honours and made nonsense of the outright competition of works and non-works bikes which signified that era. He typified the British underdog and, in spite of his often cutting comments on works boys who had it easy, seemed to enjoy, as Minter did, his underprivileged position as a pro without a works ride.

John talks straight. When he doesn't like something or considers an injustice has been done he says so. When Dave Degens and Charlie Freeman were both suspended by the ACU it was Cooper who came out openly to condemn the decision and took action to try and get the ACU to change its mind. When circuit organisers argued over the cost of providing additional straw bales to the Armco barriers John's rejoinder of 'Well if you'll be the ones to tell the parents of the lad that's killed on them, because you were too mean to provide straw bales there, I'll agree to your decision' worked. He got the straw bales.

His quotes on paddock facilities are famous the race game over.

Other famous quotes: 'Good blokes kept me off works bikes because they knew I could give them a hard time if I got one ... The insulting money offered by organisers of world championship racing and the fact that you have to queue like a pig to collect the pittances are two good reasons for not contesting the series ... Organisers get the crowds too easily and the crowd is cheated by a world championship tag ... When the going gets tough, the tough gets going.'

Not surprisingly, perhaps, he has little sentiment for the world championships. He doesn't consider them very representative, says they mean little, and gets angry when he talks about the shabby treatment of riders.

Being so successful at a time when many fans considered him a has-been, set no fire alight inside big John. He took it calmly – as though he had always known it could happen. He told me: 'I was of course pretty successful from about 1964 to 1967, the best years probably being '65 and '66, but then I had a bit of a lean time, mainly due to uncompetitive machinery. Then, when I hit on the idea of the Yamsel 350, which was extremely competitive and gave me a fresh start in the 350 class, my luck began to come in once more and the BSA 750 seemed to give me a new lease of life.'

He told me with uncommon frankness that he never thought he would win the Ontario event. 'I went out to the States feeling that I could do well and I went out with a good team to back me up. This proved worth while as the results showed.' John praises the Americans for their track facilities and says there is a lot Britain can learn from them. 'There are large, light garages to work in, a fleet of ambulances and staff ever at the ready, fire-fighting men touring the paddock on bikes, plenty of AMA officials around to answer queries, and the onlookers who like to fiddle with the bikes, ask questions and collect autographs are allowed round only after the race, not during preparation. For pre-practice and pre-race instruction and even down to the enthusiasm of the starter, the Americans take some beating.'

Cooper continued: 'The only damper came of course when the race was over and a bloke came along and said he wanted to buy my winning bike – I'm sure Steve, our BSA mechanic, would have murdered anyone who had tried to take his pride and joy away.' (A curious ruling of the Ontario event is that the winner's bike can be claimed by a prospective buyer).

'It was a relief when he agreed to buy a brand new bike. That, really, is the only criticism I have. To me the rule about buying the winner's bike is stupid and senseless and should be deleted from the AMA rule book. I am sure that Giacomo Agostini will never race in the States until something is done about it. Can you imagine MV taking the risk of someone buy-

Bill Ivy demonstrates his spectacular style during the Dutch TT
of 1969

The glamour world of Bill Ivy – honour and flowers in Japan

Gunning for victory as Jim Redman races the 250 Honda 6 round Ramsey hairpin

Owen Greenwood with his controversial mini-racer leads the conventional outfit of Charlie Freeman at Mallory Park

Phil Read with new style crash hat and colourful leathers leaps
Ballaugh Bridge in the 1971 350 cc TT

Dave Degens shows the style of a champion as he leads the
pack at Brands hatch in 1966

The incomparable Hailwood
demonstrates the excitement
and glamour of racing in the
'sixties. *Left:* Flower-power
tomfoolery at Snetterton and . . .

. . . winning the 250 cc Ulster Grand Prix in 1967

ing their bike for a little over a £1,000 – it is just ludicrous.'

American racers are wise to this claiming rule and have worked out a system to get around it with riders 'claiming' each others bikes so that everyone ends up as they started. John and Doug Hele were not of course included in the system and when buyer Bob Bailey came along with a cheque for 2,500 dollars there was little they could do, even though the BSAs market value was about five times that amount.

But in the end Bailey settled for a new bike and Coop kept his winning mount.

In 1971 end-of season offers came in from all over the world for the 33 year old John Cooper, stalwart of the 'sixties. At last he was a hot property, a sizzling success after more than a decade of dedication to home circuit racing. He turned them all down, preferring to stay home to give time to his garage business. It was a typical Cooper reaction – feet planted firmly on the ground, refusing to be moved from a commonsense line of action even in the face of success so overwhelming to unbalance the most level-headed of riders.

John Cooper weathered many crises and finally defied his critics. He kept riding and racing when everybody said he was finished. He proved them wrong, himself right and eventually beat the world . . . as he always said he could.

# 4

# The Tragedy of Fritz

Switzerland's Fritz Scheidegger was the victim of his own ambition. Twice world sidecar champion he wanted to take the title just once more. But on the way to a hat-trick, the race game claimed him.

At thirty-six years of age he was near to retirement. One more world title was all he asked. Then he would call it a day. At the Mallory Park Easter meeting in 1967 the highly respected Fritz, with sidecar passenger John Robinson, topped the bill in competition with such established British stars as Owen Greenwood, Chris Vincent and Colin Seeley. He started well. Began to make ground. He recorded the fastest lap. Then, unaccountably, disaster. Spectators watched in horror as Fritz, going into the hairpin, seemed unable to pull back. His brakes appeared to fail. Within seconds the gleaming BMW outfit had careered at speed into the barrier and Scheidegger, gentleman Fritz, was killed.

Fritz was a great champion and one of the sport's finest men. He was respected as a person and admired as a racer. Born in 1930 he was over 6 feet tall, wore glasses, spoke English well, seldom lost his temper and always projected sincerity, friendliness and honesty. Switzerland is noted for outstanding sidecar racers, but it was gentleman Fritz Scheidegger, in 1965, who broke the four year run of world championship success in the 500 cc category by Max Deubel of West Germany, also on a BMW combination. Fritz had been impressive in solo events before turning to sidecars and, in 1957, became Swiss Champion in the 350 cc and 500 cc classes, as well as securing the sidecar title for both road racing and grass tracks.

But fate is no respecter of persons. At Mallory it singled Fritz out and demanded the ultimate sacrifice. Fate again, only a year before, had cruelly attacked him when he competed in the TT races. He was at the centre of one of the sport's most sensational dramas. Four hours after winning the 130 mile sidecar TT by less than a second from Germany's Max Deubel, the Auto-Cycle Union ruled his victory out of order and disqualified him.

Fritz was alleged to have infringed the fuel regulations. Scheidegger, calm and gentle, was bitterly disappointed and resentful. He vowed that unless he was ultimately declared the winner he would never race again.

The rules were explicit. They said that unless a rider was contracted to a fuel company he must use the petrol supplied at the meeting. On his own admission Fritz did not do this, but in his own defence he said that this possible infringement had come up at the scrutineering, and nothing had been said about it.

'I have been racing for sixteen years and have always observed the rules, and now this happens. I cannot understand it,' he complained. Everyone sympathised with Scheidegger as he told his story. He said that for years he had been under contract to Castrol for oil. They had helped him early in his career so he stayed with them, but for petrol he had no contract, so first he went to get it from the refuelling tanker at the TT, but no one would let him have any. As a result he bought Esso Golden in Douglas. 'I use this petrol in all continental races,' he explained and, dejectedly, went on: 'It is pump fuel which I am sure complied with the FIM regulations. I did all the practising on Esso and adjusted the carburation for it.'

Fritz's integrity was never in doubt. It was certain that he had, as he said, declared his use of Esso Golden at the scrutineering. Auto-Cycle Union officials had checked his declaration card and said nothing. The blow came a few hours after Fritz's victory, when the ACU telephoned him to say he was not the winner. A demoralised Fritz could only say: 'This is not good for the sport. I cannot see that I have broken any regulations, but I am a rider who must work all hours on my machine, not a lawyer.'

It was all the more agonising because Fritz had already declared that he would retire at the end of the season. Because of his reputation as a racer and as a gentleman everyone desperately wanted these final few months to be a happy and successful conclusion to Scheidegger's fine career.

Fritz's story was indeed confirmed by an ACU official who also said that action had been forced on them because someone had made an official complaint. The clerk of the course, in such circumstances, would have no alternative but to disqualify Scheidegger.

To lose a race on a technicality of this kind was criminal and unjust in human terms. Fritz and John Robinson decided to fight the verdict and lodged an official protest. Everyone felt confident that, once all the facts had been established, Fritz would be reinstated as world champion. Astonishingly, an international jury meeting in Douglas on Scheidegger's case turned down his appeal after a meeting lasting three hours.

It was a severe blow for the Swiss ace. He worried about what the people back in Switzerland might think. He declared: 'This is very bad for my business in Switzerland because the people there will think I have done something very wrong, like taking dope.'

He feared that they might think he had been banned from racing so, while his natural reaction was to retire immediately, he was so dismayed and disillusioned that he decided to contest the remaining races that year. British fans were upset that such a disaster could befall Fritz Scheidegger of all people and solidly voiced their support. They were alarmed and shocked when the Douglas jury turned down his appeal, and quickly said so. Said Fritz: 'I have been very impressed by the way the British enthusiasts have supported and encouraged John Robinson and me since this trouble started, but I have not changed my mind about stopping racing. I will definitely retire at the end of the year.'

Made with such conviction at the time, events were to show how Scheidegger reversed his decision, in the way that the Isle of Man decision was reversed in the end, but with tragic result.

In the meantime, however, Fritz got the Swiss Racing Federation to take up his case. They appealed to the FIM. By early November, six months after the TT race which started it all, a meeting of RAC stewards was held in London and after a hearing lasting an hour the verdict was given in favour of Fritz and John.

Delighted with the outcome, Fritz's interest in racing was reawakened. He felt happier at the possibility of racing again, in spite of his statement about retirement. At home in Switzerland, during the close season, Scheidegger fought ill-health. He also fought against the strong urge to retire. Two world titles were his and the prospect of a third to a racer as dedicated as Fritz Scheidegger was a challenge he finally just wasn't able to reject. He began to feel better, talked to John Robinson about the possibilities, and together they decided that they would go for that third world title. Their BMW outfit was as powerful and reliable as ever. Their skill was still sharp. They could feel confident that they had every chance of notching that third world win; then Fritz could retire, content with a remarkable racing record behind him.

It was not to be. Call it unfair, tragic, catastrophic. It was all these things and race fans everywhere ranted against the circumstances which had taken Fritz from them. But they were left to mourn his passing just the same.

John Robinson was severely injured in Scheidegger's fatal crash and announced his immediate retirement. He escaped with his life and at the time of writing was reported living in Switzerland and working as a lorry driver on long hauls between the EFTA countries.

# 5

# King — But no Work's Ride

In 1964 I was working with a publisher who wanted to bring
out a book about a motor cycle racing star. Biographies in the
sport were at that time uncommon, though a superficially treated
life-story by the great Bob McIntyre had sold sufficiently well
for them to want a follow-up.

I asked Murray Walker about it. He confirmed that my
choice was straightforward and obvious. 'Derek Minter is your
man,' he declared. Little more than a year later Derek's *Racing
All My Life*, fanfared by extracts in the motor cycle press, was
on sale at track-side bookshops and booksellers throughout the
country. By this time, as forthcoming events were to show,
Derek had passed his peak as a racing star, but the book was
well presented and sold out.

Minter, for years the uncrowned King of Brands, made the
title officially his in 1965 when Brands Hatch started an annual
King of Brands feature race, the title going to the winner of this
one event. Derek rode with superb control and style. In an
outstanding display of racing, he outclassed all opposition on
his Ray Petty-tuned Norton. With ease he won the King of
Brands event and scored impressive victories in the 350 cc and
500 cc races as well.

Fifty thousand fans crowded the famous Kent circuit for that
special Good Friday meeting. Since first riding there in 1955
against the now legendary Geoff Duke, Derek had become
their home-based hero. He had developed his skills and daring
there, and had gained his fame in front of the Brands Hatch
crowds. They reflected in Minter's glory. When later, for his
own long-term good he should have been gaining wider experience competing abroad in the world classics, he chose to
stay home and race at Brands.

It was a tactical error for which Derek paid dearly. It robbed him of the opportunity to become really great, internationally.

Minter gave everything to those early races and when former 'King' John Surtees had moved on to racing cars, Derek was ready to take over. Murray Walker christened him the new 'King' over the public address system and the fans were eager to accept Derek as their own.

For six years there was no rider to match Minter at Brands Hatch. He was their biggest draw, reputed for his slow starts and devastating finishes. His fame as the King of Brands spread even to the Continent. Then, seeing the commercial potential in a special feature race for the *official* title, the Brands Hatch authorities made Minter fight for his title, putting him in open competition, with his crown at stake. In one specific race each year he would now have to prove he was 'King'.

That Good Friday in 1965 he did so conclusively. Against the top competition of Phil Read, Dave Degens and Bill Ivy, he roared away at the start. Nobody could catch him. He over-hauled similar opposition, plus the might of Mike Hailwood, to take the 350 cc event. He led all the way to score an outstanding victory in the 500 cc event. He put up the fastest lap of the day at 88 mph. It was all an incredible achievement.

A year later, defending his crown, Derek had to retire with engine trouble and Bill Ivy took the title. 'The Mint's' greatest days were over. The next year he retired.

Minter as a racing star was a dogmatic individual, cussed and stubborn, but with a breezy, cheeky personality you couldn't help but like. Fans loved him. Officials respected him but treated him warily. Contemptuous of most things, but particularly opposition riders, Minter on form and at the peak of his career was a racer of remarkable style. He was compact and efficient, a perfectionist, but a real flyer. His lap record of 90.34 mph at Brands Hatch on a Gilera in 1963 was not bettered for the next five years. When you also consider that the machine was powered by a 1958 engine, you have some measure of the man. It took the best of other top riders six and seven years to improve on many of Minter's other race and lap records.

Some of Minter's greatest rides were astride a Gilera in the 1960s. He won the British Championship on the Italian machine and, again on the Gilera, unofficially cracked John Surtees lap record at Monza. At 120.75 mph he was more than 1.5 mph faster. The very next day, in practice, Derek recorded 121 mph.

Long after Gilera retired from racing in 1957 Minter pinned his hopes on their return to full competition. While he was writing *Racing All My Life* I visited him at his modern bungalow at Blean, in Kent, and even then, as late as 1964, he continued to talk about the possibility of a Gilera revival and his part in it.

He even flew to Italy in an attempt to persuade the factory to let him have a machine to race, but the sad fact was that Gilera just didn't want to know. He was more dependent on Gilera than they on him, and the mission was unsuccessful.

Derek officially retired after the last meeting of the season at Brands Hatch on October 22, 1967, and to the end he put faith in Gilera. By this time he had already sold his beloved 500 Norton. He asked Gilera if they could provide him with a machine for his last ride. They said no – and gave as their reason that they were preparing for the Milan Show. Rebuked many times by the Italian factory, he firmly believes to this day that had he not broken his wrist in the 1966 TT they would have provided him with a ride. I doubt it and as events proved, Derek backed the wrong horse when he put his money on Gilera.

It was unfortunate, but Derek had little alternative. With Honda rides all spoken for, where else could he turn?

In February, 1966 it was reliably reported that Gilera had agreed to lend four-cylinder works machines to the promoters of Italy's early meetings at Riccione, Cesenatico, Imola and Cervia. Within twenty-four hours, the famous Italian factory changed its mind.

Derek was a brilliant rider. To see him plough his way through the field from one of his traditionally bad starts, relentlessly overhauling rider after rider, was to witness one of the most thrilling and magnificent spectacles in motor cycle racing.

At Oulton Park on August Monday in 1962 Minter broke his own lap record at a speed of 92.86 mph and in so doing became the first rider to win the 500 cc British Championship three times, '58, '61, '62. Incredibly, Derek was still a hospital outpatient at the time, attending physiotherapy four times a week following a recent crash! Minter went on to take the Championship twice more in successive seasons, establishing an outstanding record of being 500 cc British Champion five times.

Sadly Derek Minter never fully realised his potential internationally. His insistence on competing mainly in home events apart, he suffered for his own ill-timed and outspoken comments, and his disinclination to fit into a works team. As he himself once put it: 'I've won all the wrong races.'

That is not quite true. He rode superbly, many times, to win races of major tactical importance which should have brought him a long-term works contract at his own price... but somehow the really big chance never came.

It should have come after his epic 100 mph lap on a Norton in the 1960 Senior TT – the first-ever by any rider on a single-cylinder British machine.

It should have come after his victory on a Norton against John Surtees on a powerful MV at Brands Hatch.

It should have come most of all in 1962 when 'The Mint' was spectacularly successful in almost everything he did. He entered as many as five races in an afternoon, against the toughest opposition, and won everything. He secured a treble victory at Oulton Park, shattered records at Castle Coombe, saw everybody off at Brands Hatch, collected 1,000 guineas at Mallory Park for winning the big race there, and was voted 'Man of the Year' by readers of *Motor Cycle News*.

If this wasn't enough to put him into a works team, then what was? The TT surely. Derek pressed his claim in the most positive way any rider could: he won the 250 cc event with a remarkable display of riding.

Again, in a moment of outstanding triumph, everything went wrong. He was passed over. Riding a privately entered one-year-old Honda, he committed the unforgivable sin of out-riding the works team with their brand new Hondas and elaborate support system of managers, mechanics and spares. Honda didn't appreciate him making them look foolish and at later times when they were looking for someone to offer a contract to, and Minter was available, the choice fell elsewhere.

Although I suspect Derek would never forsake a moment of glory against the possibility of securing the future, he complained bitterly. 'They said I flung away my chance of a work's ride because I disobeyed signals to slow down and let the team members through.'

Technically, Derek couldn't be faulted. He was riding for Hondis Ltd., the British Concessionaires for Honda at the time, and he insisted that they gave him no instructions to ease back to let the works boys take the glory.

'I just went on to win,' he said. 'I have always done my best. I don't back-pedal for anyone.' Derek told *Motor Cycle News*: 'It was not my fault the Honda works riders could not keep up with me, and there is no reason why I should have given up my chance of winning to save their faces.'

Talking about the incident to me in 1971 Derek was still bitter though his comments had mellowed with the passing years. 'When I look back, I think I might have been given a warning, but I didn't realise it at the time. Before the race, as we were lining up for the start, the Honda team manager came over to me. We were about to push off. I remember him saying: 'Don't forget, Jim's leading the world championship.' I didn't think anything of it at the time. I was too keyed up ready for the race. But I suppose it could have been interpreted as a warning that I had to let Jim Redman win.'

Had he at the time realised the comment for what it was, it is still hardly likely he would have taken notice of it. As he himself said, he didn't back pedal for anyone and 'The Mint' in full flight was very much his own master. He picked his own races, negotiated his own fees, fought his own battles, and said what he felt.

He criticised organisers for delaying their final selection until a rider who had been left out couldn't find another event. He criticised promoters for giving works riders too much starting money. 'So they attract the crowds' he conceded, 'but are they worth the vast sums paid to them by promoters, bearing in mind that they have all their expenses paid? They could afford to have their money cut so that there was a little more for the non-works boys, struggling against the high cost of maintaining bikes and travelling to meetings.' He criticised the top riders who borrowed old works machinery. He called it dishonest. 'The promoter and the crowd are entitled to think that they'll see a current machine, not a model from a few years back, even though it might still blow off all the local lads.'

Habitually, he attacked the TT, complaining there was far too little money in it to make the trip worthwhile.

Minter, talking in 1967: 'After my practice crash last year, someone stole £70 from my pocket while I was in hospital. Most riders lose money by riding in the TT, but that was the last straw. I'm definitely not going this year or ever again, unless I get a work's ride and have to.' Derek estimated his practice crash had cost him around £2,000 in all. 'It's just too expensive for a professional without a work's ride. If things go well it's bad enough. If things go wrong it's impossible.' Other racers felt the same way but kept their mouths shut.

Irish fans were up in arms when his book was published. Of the Dundrod circuit, home of the Ulster Grand Prix, he wrote: 'How it wins international status I'll never know. It is raced on public highway roads which are worse than some of the most neglected rural roads in this country. In the paddock you have to start up your bicycles on shingle, and the toilet facilities are just a joke – hopsack tied round some stakes.' He also attacked the organisation: 'There always seems to be plenty of people in authority rushing around but really knowing very little about what is going on.' But that, of course, was written in 1965.

In the early days he took pride and enjoyed fame in being the outstanding 'home' rider. His exceptional technique made him master of the short circuits, and in Britain he was supreme. He was less comfortable overseas, on tracks with long 'burn up' straights, where his personal Nortons found the going harder against the more powerful works-prepared machines of people like Hailwood, Ivy and Agostini. Galloping round Brands as a star attraction and with a good chance of winning would bring him more fans and more ready cash than a trip to East Germany, for instance. Without a works contract to give him security and take care of the considerable travel and hotel expenses, his decision to stay at home seemed right and sensible at the time. Too late he realised his mistake; he tried repeatedly to persuade a factory to sponsor him, but without success.

Derek came up the tough way. He battled for his success. Temperamentally individual he decided to sort out problems for himself, plan his own course. He was left to make up his own mind, right or wrong. When this is the way it is, you can't afford to be over-charitable to the opposition, or grant them too much talent. Derek's comments on other riders are, there-fore, predictably terse and to the point...Ivy – *a real goer*; Agostini – *a good runner*; Hailwood – *money bought him the best bikes*. On equal machinery he considered himself a match for Hailwood at any time.

Minter was undoubtedly the most outstandingly successful short-circuit road racer of his generation – possibly of all times. He had immense talent. He should have been a factory rider for most of his career, but the tragedy was he could never fit into a team for long. He felt deeply and honestly about racing, and was just too candid with his comments for his own good. The fans loved him for it, but the fans don't pick the works teams, fix the races or pay the money. In the end the Brands Hatch fans let him down shamefully.

The trouble was that Derek, as a 'privateer' did everything himself. He was too busy racing to organise the business side of his career properly. Now he regrets it. 'I ought to have competed in the classics instead of rushing round Brands so much. Maybe I should have kept my mouth shut a bit more often too,' he says with a wry smile.

I doubt if he could have done. Even now, as he looks back on his own racing days, the uncompromising views come through strongly. 'The old friendliness has gone. When I was racing, blokes would loan you a spare or two if you were stuck. The standard of riding has dropped. There is very little chance now for a talented youngster to make racing a full-time career, so he doesn't get the opportunity to improve himself. That's one reason why speeds haven't gone up as they should have done. TT speeds should be well up in the 100s – yet the stretch up to Ballacraine is only about 5 seconds quicker now than when I last rode there. At Brands I was lapping at 90 on a Norton. What are they doing now?' Derek said he was told he was an idiot to ride the Villiers Starmaker-engined Cotton. 'I didn't listen,' he said, 'and look what happened. When I proved it could go, Villiers took it over themselves and Cotton and I got the sack.'

Minter in full racing song was sheer poetry in motion. No one rode a bike with such immaculate ease. He looked a born rider, but he always insisted that champion riders were not born, but made. 'It takes hours of study, practice and experiment finding the best way. Speed is the last thing you worry about . . . and don't be afraid of being called chicken,' he advised youngsters. He never took to the 'knees out' technique, but rather dismissed it as a piece of unnecessary showmanship which had little to do with good riding.

He suffered serious crashes, broke collar bones, wrist, nose and back. Yet he was a safe rider, never taking a chance, having no part in the cut and thrust of the battling which can go on at the bends. He was also a perfectionist: 'Riders these days don't study their machines or the circuits nearly enough. I knew Brands, Oulton and the others better than I knew the layout of my own bungalow. There's more to racing on motor cycles than belting round on full cog.'

Had a factory signed him to a long-term contract, and had Derek controlled his uncompromising nature, there is no doubt he could have become one of the world's greatest motor cycle racers. Whether he would have been as happy, or whether we would have had as much respect for him, is a very different matter.

On the few occasions he did ride competitive machinery on foreign circuits, he showed how devastating he could be, and to this day he considers his greatest race to be his victory on a Gilera at Imola in 1963. He had never before been to the circuit, but after a reasonable start came through to win from such class opposition as John Hartle (Gilera) and Mike Hailwood (MV).

Derek rode his retirement race at Brands Hatch in October, 1967. He celebrated with scintillating wins in the 350 cc and 1000 cc events and was only two lengths behind in the 500 cc final. Then 'The Mint' was gone. And Brands Hatch hasn't been quite the same since.

When he retired he said there just weren't enough big meetings in Britain to make it all worth while any more.

He now has very little contact with the race game. He told me: 'When I turned up at Brands Hatch some time ago a marshall there didn't even know who I was. I was mad. I said to him: "Have you heard of a chap called Derek Minter?" "Yeah, I've heard of him!" said the marshall – "So what?" I just walked away in disgust.'

'Motor cycles have filled so much of my life that I still get the urge to keep close to the game. I'd like to be a team manager.' That ambition, like the works contract and his Gilera hopes, is hardly likely to be fulfilled unless many more opportunities become available.

A cabinet full of trophies and his old leathers remind Minter of his most glorious moments – along with Jenny, once a fan in the paddock at Brands and now his wife.

To remind us we have the vivid recollection of Derek's barnstorming action in snatching the 250 cc TT from under the noses of the Honda works boys, a titanic achievement. Remember? Hailwood and Minter moved off first, Derek trailing as they went down Bray Hill. Then Tom Phillis was away, followed by Dan Shorey, Alan Shepherd, Bob McIntyre, Jim Redman and the others. Minter takes the lead, but Phillis, coming up with a fierce turn of speed, rushes ahead of both Hailwood and McIntyre, though Mac moved into second place behind Minter a little later on. At the end of the first lap, McIntyre is ahead with a lap speed of 99.06 mph from a standing start. Redman is second and Minter is third.

The second lap saw the retirement through engine trouble of McIntyre and in lap 3, with several other riders out because of mechanical failure, the race is beginning to sort itself out. Minter is now travelling very fast indeed, but he loses ground when he pulls in to refuel, overshoots and has to wheel the Honda back to the pits.

Into the fourth lap and half the race gone, Derek restarts from the pits only seconds behind Redman. Jim is moving fast, but Minter is riding the race of his life and at the start of lap 5 is leading Redman. As Jim pulls in to refuel, Derek storms ahead and into the lead on corrected time. Redman blasts off from the pits, streaking in pursuit of Minter. But 'The Mint' is really travelling and in spite of Jim's challenge continues to pull away.

As riders race through into the final lap Minter is going with incredible power, but Redman is in trouble. He pulls into the pits again, complaining that the filler cap on his Honda keeps opening and spraying him with petrol. Hailwood on a troublesome Benelli is now riding without faring, but not for long. There is a splutter, the engine dies, and Mike has lost all interest in the race. His devoted fans are now confident of a

Minter win but there is still that final lap to be completed. Only mechanical failure or some kind of accident can rob Derek of the title now. He continues to ride beautifully ... and rides on, against all odds, to win one of the most momentous races in the history of motor cycle sport.

Minter suffered for his outspoken comments, but it is significant that his criticisms of the TT was still being sounded ten years after by other equally famous riders. In *Motor Cycle News*, John Cooper, for instance, bitterly attacked the TT. 'I don't like the TT's cash set-up' he complained. 'Hotels, ferries and car firms make thousands from the TT, but don't seem to put anything into it directly. I'm sorry for the poor bloke who goes to the island to race, then breaks down and can hardly afford to get home. It's not good enough not to get at least the boat fare paid.'

Nobody is interested in a fallen idol – or a motor cycle racer once he's gone. Brands, to their credit, held a benefit meeting for Derek shortly after he retired. Here was the chance for thousands of fans to pay tribute to a 'King' they had cherished for years, but memory is extraordinarily short and such affairs never seem to enjoy the support they deserve. Reflecting on the occasion, Derek smiled ruefully: 'When you're not winning or you've done your bit, people don't want to know anymore. For years I'd been the biggest draw at Brands, but the crowds didn't bother to turn out when I had my benefit and I finished up with less than £100.'

Times change. New heroes take the place of old. But this shameful treatment of Derek Minter, at the hands of his own fans, must surely rank as one of motor cycle racing's most sickening injustices ever.

# 6

# High-flying Obsession

Fred Cooper lived with an obsession. He dreamed of becoming the fastest man in the world on two wheels. Against exceptional odds, working on a scratch budget with only marginal help and virtually no financial support, he toiled away in the finest traditions of Britain's 'garden shed' inventors. Yet Cooper lived in a modern world where money was power and things happen fast.

The Americans held the record and were determined to keep it. Before Cooper had qualified for the support that would have brought him a fair crack at the title, the chance had gone. Now the dream lies shattered and Fred Cooper, his driving ambition extinguished by circumstance, is left to contemplate an ultimate world record which might so easily have been his.

Fred's big chances were in 1968 and '69. The official record stood to American Bill Johnson at 224.57 mph, set up in 1962 at Utah in a steamlined Triumph with a 649 cc twin engine. Bent not only in capturing the official title for Britain, Cooper was also out to beat the 245.667 mph unofficial record of American Bob Leppan in his spectacular Gyronaut projectile in 1966, which had the same type engines but not super charged as Cooper's. He was confident he could do it. 'My bike is capable of 190 mph without further streamlining,' he claimed.

The news brought the *Daily Express* hot foot on the scene and their motor sport reporter Leslie Nichol outlined a spectacular scheme which he hoped would give Cooper the help he needed.

Fred was invited to Fleet Street to see *Express* editor Tim Hewitt and after the meeting came away thrilled and excited with the promise of substantial support for his project. Prospects looked good then, but the deal hinged on Fred Cooper proving he was the man to lead Britain back to world speed glory.

First he must reach 200 mph in *this* country. Then, and only then, would they sponsor his attempt at the title at Bonneville Salt Flats in the United States.

It looked to be an outstanding opportunity and the motor cycle world buzzed with excitement. Fred's fantastic 1300 cc double Triumph twin powered Cyclotron was a good, basic machine, and the target of 200 mph seemed reasonable enough. Hadn't George Brown, for instance, on his 1000 Vincent-powered super Nero sped near to that mark on a number of occasions? Alf Hagon also had his ambitions set somewhere in that speed bracket.

Precedent helped Cooper's ultimate goal little. The only British bid for the title to be staged in America was in 1949 when Noel Pope on a 1000 cc Brough Superior tried and failed. Yet everything was so different in the 'sixties. For Britain it was a time of tremendous excitement and pace. We had entered the swinging era of the Beatles, London fashions were sweeping the world, the *Backing Britain* Campaign was gaining momentum, and for the first time since the dark days of the war, everything seemed to be going for the old country.

Could Fred jump on the bandwagon and gain a world title for Britain? The opportunity looked outstanding. The *Express* support seemed generous enough and the paper appeared determined to apply a solid shoulder to help get the project moving. *Motor Cycle* reported: 'The paper is ready to finance the 200 mph British bid and pay for a special cigar shell and a trip to Utah. There will be no half measures. Negotiations are going on for the use of Fairford RAF station, Gloucestershire, earmarked for testing the Concorde airliner.'

FIM international timekeepers were to be arranged to supervise the attempt which, if successful, would clear the way for the making of the streamlined shell vital to Fred's serious challenge in the USA.

Good support had been promised and Fred Cooper, his reputation already established through two world titles, the one-mile standing-start and the 500 cc quarter-mile, had the courage and experience to pull it off. A reported quote from Leslie Nichol added to the drama: 'We will have the cigar designed at Farnborough aircraft research establishment. The

C

best brains in Britain will be working on the attempt.'

Our chances looked bright and the timing was ideal. No one seriously believed that even if we could take the title we would hold on to it for long. American speed stars, backed by massive commercial resources and the best facilities, would soon once again be clamouring for time at Bonneville in an effort to push the record higher. Britain had to move quickly. The chance was now, and however fleeting, what glory the world title would bring to a country desperate for international honours.

But first, that qualifying 200 mph must be reached and, tragically for British sporting prestige, Fred's assault was destined to founder there. In the delirium of a possible crack at a world speed title, the comparatively simple job of attaining the qualifying speed had been relegated to something of a trifling formality. The real business would be out in America in a few months' time.

But sadly, Fred never made 200.

He struggled painfully to reach the speed which would give him the big chance. His first attempt didn't materialise, he suffered mechanical problems on his second try, and bad weather shattered the third. In the meantime, the *Backing Britain* campaign was beginning to lose its bite, *Daily Express* editor Tim Hewitt left Fleet Street for Australia, the newspaper's enthusiasm was not unnaturally blowing itself out with the inevitable decline of the *Backing Britain* campaign, and as Fred Cooper's elusive 200 mph seemed to grow further away than ever.

The Fairford attempt, news of which had rocketed Cooper into the headlines, was never held because unexpected difficulties arose during efforts to secure the use of the runways. We had great hopes again at Honington in June 1968 when Fred clocked 185 mph before a rear crankshaft sheared on his sixth and final run. He wasn't too despondent, but pleaded: 'I need a streamlined shell.' What was much more demoralising for Cooper was Alf Hagon's claim three months later that his supercharged 1230 cc Hagon-JAP Special had touched 206.54 mph on a one-way run.

A hard-pressed and frustrated Cooper couldn't believe it and even four years later looked back incredulously. 'How he managed 200 I'll never know,' he told me.

Mentally bruised by Hagon's claim, Cooper battled on. In March 1969 a further attempt was planned at Duxford airfield in Essex, a venue far from ideal. Only 1½ miles long, it would give Fred little enough room for braking after building up the revs to pass through the time trap at all possible speed. Cooper was conscious of the problems, but not demoralised by them. He said: 'Even with the *Express* behind me it's going to take a tremendous effort to get the bike to America this year. But if everyone co-operates I'm hoping we can make it and push the record way out of the Americans' reach.'

The plan was for Fred, the 200 mph successfully outpaced, to travel to Bonneville for the speed week in September, only six months ahead. A frantic race to prepare the machine for the record bid was anticipated. A streamlined shell, totally necessary for such an attempt, would have to be designed, constructed, wind-tunnel tested and fitted to Fred's machine, which itself would need modifications to accommodate the shell. A crack at the world title, however, would be reward enough.

At this crucial point fate, as at Fairford and Honington, once again took control. The day chosen for the 200 mph qualifying attempt dawned grey and bleak. Fred's mood was similarly gloomy when he woke and saw the weather. Charlie Rous of *Motor Cycle News* telephoned to say that snow was falling at Duxford. Cooper, bitterly disappointed, didn't even bother to go. At what might easily have been one of the most significant moments in British motor cycle history, snow covered the Duxford runway and the hero of the piece sat brooding at home.

It was a melancholy time because under the auspices of the *Daily Express* Fred had already made his final bid. He was not to have another chance. Even before Duxford the spirit and adventure which had roused the motor cycle world to a new level of expectancy when the compelling scheme had been announced little more than a year before was already draining away. Duxford crucified it. There was no formal closure to the *Daily Express* offer, but there was little doubt that the sting had gone from it. A miracle was needed to give it meaning again, but the miracle didn't come and Britain's big chance was gone.

Ironically, had Cooper been able to squeeze the world title from the Americans during '69, he would have become out-

right world speed champion for at least three years, for even in
1972 and in spite of unofficial speed records, Bill Johnson's
224.57 mph remained the *official* fastest in the world.

Fred Cooper, grateful at the time for the support promised
by the *Daily Express*, wishes now they could have done more.
Their motives were honourable, the desire was there, but he
firmly believes they underestimated the size and complexity of
the undertaking they pledged to support. He told me: 'They
said they would help find a suitable place for the 200 mph run.
After pushing out advance publicity about Fairford, they
weren't able to sort out all the problems connected with getting
approval. I don't think they fully realised, for instance, how
costly insurance cover can be when a speed test of this kind
is run on an airfield. Certainly they did well to get Honington,
but Duxford was far from ideal and even if I had made the
attempt there, didn't really give me much of a chance.'

Cooper, disappointed and disillusioned at the time, has since
become embittered over what he described as a pathetic response to his pleas for help from the motor cycle trade. 'In the
end I simply got fed up with begging,' he complained. 'Leslie
Nichol scrounged two engines for me from Triumph and I was
grateful to him for that. The engines were not as one may think
a special highly tuned pair of engines. They were the basic
main parts of an obsolete type engine. If it had been possible
for me to have been given the latest three cylinder engines
which were being produced there would have been no doubt
at all as to the speeds I could have reached. Champion and
Renolds coughed up with plugs and chains, Dunlop supplied
me with special tyres and offered to look after them, but when
it came to handing out cash bonuses the amount I was told
they could give was £50 . . . and that only after I had brought
the world speed title back to Britain! The *Express* sponsorship
was a tremendous boost. More support from the industry to help
me reach 200 and I'm convinced I could have done it. After all,
at Elvington I averaged 194 mph over the Kilo, a world record
for a 1300 machine, and travelled well in excess of 200 in order
to get this average speed. It still could be done by Britain, if
people would only put up the money.'

How near Fred Cooper came to establishing a world record
nobody can accurately say. It seems clear, however, that he

perhaps came closer, potentially, than many people fully realised at the time and given the opportunity over again, knowing what is known now, Fred might have found a more generous attitude to his pleas for support.

As *Motor Cycle News* editor Robin Miller commented: 'I think Freddie Cooper's record attempt might well have succeeded, and still might, but all these things take a lot of money and as this was virtually a one man effort he had neither the time nor the money to devote to it. Britain did, indeed, miss a first class opportunity, but when you see works-backed attempts in the States failing, then it is easy to understand how difficult it is for a one-man effort to succeed.'

Failures, however valiant, are distorted by what-might-have beens. One major doubt standing proud of all others, however, is whether, had more effort been directed specifically to helping Cooper reach the qualifying 200 mph, rather than the proposed bid in America, the outcome might have been different.

Fred Cooper, speed ace of the 'sixties and still active in less momentous situations, celebrated his 48th birthday in 1973. Is there any ambition left? A world title? 'Certainly I'd be interested, but not if it meant begging for money and scratching around for support. I'm not interested in all that again, but with the right amount of resources behind me – a Count Augusta for instance, or a Honda-type organisation – then certainly I'd have a go.'

Then plaintively: 'But I can't see it happening . . . can you?'

# 7

# The Battlefield

The 'sixties were rich in racing talent. They were also the battleground for some of the sport's most sensational dramas, public rows and angry scenes. Officialdom took a hammering. Riders retaliated against what they alleged was unjust treatment from crowds, organisers and the system. Organisers threatened bans on riders. Riders threatened a boycott of disputed events.

Never, it seemed, had the race game been quite so volatile. Angry accusations demanded uncompromising denials. British riders were the biggest names and at home and abroad claimed the biggest, boldest headlines. Monza and Brands were threatened by boycott. Stars walked out of a Cadwell meeting. Mallory faced a strike of riders, while fans, resentful of being the pawns in a power game between riders and organisers, cold shouldered the mighty Mike Hailwood at Ulster and protested with a slow handclap at Mallory.

The slow handclap highlighted something of the rift which developed during the 'sixties between the highly paid works stars and the more hard-pressed non-works riders. These were the big-money days of the factory-sponsored rider and many of those left outside this elite band felt increasingly aggrieved that too many of the most appetising carrots were being dangled in front of the globetrotting star names, leaving too few perks for themselves.

Mallory's incident was one of a number which brought these clashes out into the open in front of the fans. Of the 24 riders who qualified for the main events, 13 at first refused to race, complaining that Hailwood, Agostini, Read and Ivy were all to be paid start money, while they were not. Nothing short of an assurance from Grovewood Circuits general manager Chris Lowe that the riders would be given an opportunity to present their grievances, would pacify the reluctant, protesting competitors, who only then agreed to continue racing.

The fans, meantime, showed their displeasure in the only way they knew how ... the slow handclap.

Operating on meagre budgets, paying all their own expenses, having to plead for what sponsorship they could get and risking their necks just the same, the non-works boys certainly had a case. No one could deny it. Yet it was the glamour boys of the Grand Prix with their exotic works machinery who could pull in the biggest crowds and organisers had to recognise this fact. Big names were box-office, and the temperaments weren't always easy to handle.

The Mallory protest won the day for the non-works riders and it was decided at the subsequent meeting that for the remaining international meetings of the season start money would be paid to them though to make room for this cash awards paid to the winners would be reduced. No more cash, but a different kind of share-out.

Mallory had been at the centre of a row only a month before when riders protested about what they believed to be a drop in prize money. Circuit manager Jack Walton denied the allegation. He admitted that in March Mallory had paid out £1,500, yet in April only £990, but he explained that the April pay-out was exactly the same as the April pay-out the previous year. He told *Motor Cycle News*: 'This is normally a poor meeting and therefore we pay accordingly.' The incident showcased the tense, suspicious atmosphere which prevailed. There seemed little trust by one side in the other.

Sometimes there were serious repercussions. Two months following the Mallory strike Pat Mahoney, unable to obtain acceptance for his entries in national and international meetings, alleged victimisation. 'I'm convinced of it,' he said. The testimony put forward to substantiate his claim centred around his application to race in the Hutchinson meeting. It had been turned down. When Paul Smart's entry on the Bob Curtis 650 Norton became vacant Mahoney tried again. Again he was refused, but later the organisers agreed he could take part if he obtained permission from Smart's father, who had made the original entry. By the time this was done, official practice was over and Pat was refused permission to have a late practice session.

Answering these accusations, British Motor Cycle Racing Club secretary Jim Swift said that although Mahoney's original entry had been received before the closing date, all classes he applied for were by that time filled.

Money was the cause of many of these squabbles, including the possibility of a boycott of star riders which threatened Brands Hatch, Mallory Park, Snetterton and Oulton Park at the beginning of 1968. Motor Circuit Developments, who controlled the four circuits, had already abolished start money from national meetings in favour of increased prize money and it was the consideration of a similar plan for international meetings at the circuits that produced the threatened boycott. Mike Hailwood, Phil Read and Bill Ivy, then among the biggest names in world racing, all said they would not take part without start money.

Motor Circuit Developments admitted to such a scheme being in their minds, stating it was a logical development of the plan which they had introduced at national meetings. It would encourage non-works riders, they said. The star names accepted this, but self-interests were strong in the 'sixties and attitudes often, in the beginning, intransigent. Hailwood said he wouldn't ride unless he was given start money, and Read said he wasn't too worried as he had fixed up several starts in the early Italian meetings.

Anyone as outstandingly successful as Mike Hailwood in the 'sixties was certain to attract almost as much criticism as adulation, and the fans who spoke up against him weren't concerned with diplomacy. When he went to contest the Ulster Grand Prix in August 1967, it was evident that the squabbles over start money in which Mike had been involved prior to the race had done nothing to add to his reputation. Because of it many had quietly switched their support to Agostini and were hoping for an Italian victory over the Honda. Reported *Motor Cycle's* Mick Woollett: 'Main reason for their attitude is that the local papers heard plenty from the organisers, but very little from Hailwood, who arrived in Ulster only the day practising started. And he didn't improve matters by sending Ralph Bryans to do his final negotiating instead of facing the organisers himself. As usual in a barney of this sort, there was a lot to be said for both sides. Pity it wasn't patched up, for Mike is one of the nicest characters in the game, while the organisers of the Ulster are just about the hardest working and most enthusiastic bunch of motor cycle racing enthusiasts you could possibly meet.'

The doubtful distinction of being the rider who most upset the Ulster fans, however strongly they might have felt about Hailwood in 1967, was undoubtedly Derek Minter with comments in his book, *Racing All My Life,* published two years before. Derek was never one to phrase his complaints delicately. When he didn't like something he said so openly. He complained with remarkable frankness about road conditions at the Ulster and the general facilities and organisation.

Publication of these views caused a storm. Derek was accused of being 'only happy on nice, comfortable courses', of being too soft and cosy. A Belfast critic wrote: 'A world championship class man can ride and win on any type of road-racing circuit. With the top aces willing to compete at Dundrod, perhaps we shan't miss Derek if he would rather not come.'

Derek's fans countered strongly. They quoted his outstanding record, his obvious skill and daring. One asked Minter's critics if they would consider the TT course to be nice and comfortable, and then went on to point out that Derek's remarkable record on the Island was there for all to see.

It wasn't the first time a circuit had been hotly criticised. Only a year before a number of top class riders threatened to boycott the Italian Grand Prix at Monza because the organisers planned to include a section of the circuit which they felt to be exceptionally dangerous. The section, steeply-banked and bumpy, was claimed to be anything but a natural road racing hazard.

It was in Italy, but this time at Riccione, that tempers flared on another hotly disputed issue. It was April 1969. High starting money had reportedly been paid to the big-time stars from Britain, Mike Hailwood, Phil Read, Ralph Bryans and Stuart Graham, and the fans expected to see them riding their high-powered works machines. When they turned up with older bikes, two allegedly having been taken from a museum, an ugly situation threatened and at one point there seemed to be danger of a walk out, but for the good of the event the organisers were able to smooth things over and the races were held. Bryans won the 125 cc race, but riding such outdated machinery, Read, Graham and Hailwood weren't in the running.

Often, it seemed, there was needle and friction in Italy. In 1967 Phil Read and Bill Ivy, there to race at Cesenatico and Imola, claimed they were snubbed by the Italians, packed up their belongings and came home without competing. Said Read: 'It wasn't just a question of money. They didn't appear to want us. They simply weren't interested in any terms.'

In 1969 the Spanish Grand Prix was held at the Jarama circuit, just outside Madrid, instead of at Barcelona. Riders weren't happy about the switch. The twisty 2.2 miles circuit, though just sufficiently long to meet FIM regulations, was considered short for a world championship. Another grouse resulted from the organisers insistence in running the races in class order. With the 500 event following the 350, riders competing in both were faced with the daunting prospect of 78 laps almost non-stop. Adding to a most unsatisfactory situation was the limiting of practice to one day, and the inability of the petrol supplied by the organisers for the two-stroke riders, to mix with oil. It was only after strong protests by two-strokers Bill Ivy, Rod Gould and Jack Findlay, that the organisers agreed to provide more suitable petrol. Though riders were annoyed and disgruntled, there was on this occasion no threatened strike or boycott. The meeting went through as planned with a relentless Agostini, in spite of two falls, taking both the 350 cc and 500 cc events.

It was in 1966 that the top international road racers formed their own union. Called the World Championship Riders Association it was established to foster better relations between organisers and riders. That such an improved relationship was needed there could be little doubt, but most fans saw the Association, which was to be restricted to top-class riders who intended to contest every round of the World Championship, as a way for riders to give official backing to their grievances and campaign for their interests through a structure recognised by both sides. It was significant that one of the declared aims of the committee would be to look into complaints by riders and take them up with the organisers concerned.

The scheme won solid support from the majority of top-level riders including Mike Hailwood, Stuart Graham, Peter Williams, John Cooper, John Hartle, Ron Chandler, Hugh Anderson, Frank Perris, Phil Read and Jim Redman though, cautious of the attitude of the FIM to the scheme, it was agreed, for fear of recriminations, that the Association would not have one rider as its figure-head.

The Association would draw up an officially recognised grading list of 30 riders in each class and organisers of World Championship events would then have to accept riders in that order. This would eliminate the free-for-all system of establishing entry for such events and would help to ensure the best possible standards of racing for these important championship races. Organisers would, of course, be free to accept entries from a certain number of their own national riders.

The Association would also work to establish fixed scales for starting money at classic events for works, semi-works and private riders. Thus there would be no individual bargaining between racers and organisers.

Stated in those terms it all seemed genuine, logical and justified. On the other hand, organisers and officialdom can't have been too happy with the movement. It threatened their authority. An 'organised front' of riders could bring them problems and was certain to mean, at best, a change of attitude on their part, certain reorganisation and re-adjustment, and at worst, higher risk of friction, boycotts and a harder line generally from riders in their attitudes to race organisation.

If they lost any sleep over it, they needn't have bothered. Top class riders, when it comes down to the detail of organising themselves, find the process tedious and time-consuming. Their life is racing, and they are often too individualistic and uncompromising to work well as a team or a committee. The Association idea, which had offered so much promise, never really showed its colours or its teeth so that little more than a year later up came the idea of another kind of Association, this time to protect the interests of the Grand Prix circus elite.

Again the idea was to force a better deal from organisers and with fewer riders – some 13 against 30 in the earlier scheme – the plan seemed more manageable. Jack Findley, one of the top riders behind the scheme, explained: 'We are professionals and we feel we have the right to command greater respect.'

This time the approach was tougher from the start. If Grand Prix organisers weren't prepared to meet their terms, they wouldn't ride.

But in 1969 time was beginning to run out for the riders. The gigantic investment from which motor cycle racing had lived lavishly and spectacularly, had seen its peak. The herculian figures whose names had dominated the 'sixties and added to the substance and authority of the rider, were disappearing from the scene. Circumstances soon made it impossible, or certainly unwise, for riders to support their efforts for a better deal with talk of organised action and boycotts. Works rides were fewer, sponsorships harder to win, the cost of competing internationally as a private rider financially overwhelming. The riders' big chance had disappeared and time had swung the advantage once more to the favour of the organisers and the status quo.

Many reasons have been advanced for the failure of a riders' association, but John Brown in *Motor Cycle News* probably covered most of the reasons: 'Attempts have failed because no one was prepared to do all the work, too many people were involved and the majority wanted a lot but were prepared to do precious little to get it.'

Certainly, these points seem valid when set against the first really serious efforts to form an association in 1966–67. In the second attempt the aggressive stance taken by the riders, understandably provoked through desperation in seeing the failure of earlier efforts, did nothing to help co-operation from organisers, but more probably it was a shift in conditions within the sport which led to its collapse.

There can be no doubt that riders were often treated shamefully in the high-speed world of the 'sixties and their attempts to organise themselves were justified. One can't help feeling, however, that they might have achieved more had they been a little more diplomatic, professional and less committed almost from the start to a pitched battle with organisers. Could a professional public relations organisation, for instance, have done more, working on their behalf to a tightly prepared brief. They would have had the time, the know-how in the art of communication, and the financial incentive to work hard and intelligently on behalf of the riders. Still there would have been problems and difficulties, but the chances of winning their way with organisers might have been better.

Public relations, a dramatic phenomenon a few years ago, and now accepted all round as an important function of business life, is itself an issue which prompts controversy in motor cycle sport. There was a growing feeling in the 'sixties that motor cycle racing was not selling itself as well, or as much, as it might. Poor coverage on television and radio was seen to demonstrate the need for more positive action to give motor cycle racing a more sophisticated, up-to-date image, and a bigger corner of the market. Couldn't more be done to attract greater sponsorship? How about some new style racing, and a fresh look at old ideas. No longer was it enough to let events take a natural course. They must be channelled into pre-determined directions. Motor cycle racing, voiced the critics, was in desperate need of modern style promotion. The mass of the public should be encouraged to take an interest.

The whizz-kids who pushed for widespread change condemned the Auto-Cycle Union, who appeared jaded and sluggish by comparison. They were criticised for not doing enough, or not knowing what was needed. They were too conservative, said some, and narrow minded – out-of-touch with changing times, not sufficiently concerned with promoting the sport, too willing to sit back and simply administer a set of rules.

It is easy to poke fun at the ACU. Perhaps they could have done more, but with the mass media being subjected to increasing pressure from all sides for claims on time and attention, public relations wouldn't necessarily have been the instant fairy godmother which solved all problems, opened all doors and brought an up-to-date sparkle to the grime-edged image of motor cycle racing.

Meantime, there were more tangible issues to be debated. A row developed when the Competitions Committee of the ACU recommended an extension of the road racing season, and growing criticism threatened the reputation of the famous TTs as one of the greatest road races in the world.

By using an engine of incorrect or oversize capacity, a

rider was able to gain an unfair advantage over the opposition. Beneath the surface there had been suspicions of such irregularities for some time, but it was left to rider Dave Croxford to ram the message home with a public announcement and condemnation. The issue was taken up by tuner Steve Lancefield who maintained he knew of at least two records which had been established by engines of the wrong capacity. 'Any engine which breaks a lap, race or class record should be measured,' he declared.

To beat the bandits as they were known, the ACU announced a scheme of random checks on engine sizes for the following season. Penalty for being found guilty of this cheap kind of fraud would make a rider liable to exclusion from the results and the suspension of his licence.

Motor cycle racing attracts brave men and outstanding characters. They are often impulsive in their comments and fickle in their views. High-flying rows can develop in an instant, and disappear just as swiftly. When the ACU Competitions Committee recommended an extension of the road racing season by two months, until the end of December, opposition came immediately, not only from members of the General Council, but from many riders; and slowly, but relentlessly, feeling too was building up against the TT races and was to culminate in sensational outbursts in the early 1970s.

Against the background of what *Motor Cycle* described as 'one of the most tragic fortnights in TT history,' top riders made savage attacks on the state of the 37¾ mile circuit and what was described as the lack of willingness on the part of the Island's government to spend enough of the revenue they enjoyed through the races on making the road surface safer.

The 'sixties were to become historic as the period of Mike Hailwood. They witnessed his years of outstanding triumphs culminating in 12 TT victories and 9 world titles, but they were historic too as the time Mike chose to quit motor cycle racing.

Mike had dominated the sport and had been at the flashpoint of many of its disturbances. His moneyed background and the massive support he received from Honda weren't calculated to win him the warm affection the fans reserve for the under-dog. Yet who could criticise him for making use of the natural opportunities open to him and there for the taking. To his credit, he often refused to be drawn into petty squabbles, but in 1966 he was driven to answer his critics in an open letter published in *Motor Cycling*. Said Hailwood: 'The knockers obviously think that I go to meetings with the deliberate inten-tion of breaking down, getting punctures or of not even starting in races, because I'm frightened of getting beaten. I'm not making excuses. I don't think I have to. I am just sick to death of being the target of a lot of uncalled-for abuse every week.'

Good for Mike. His track record was phenomenal and, as he said, did his critics think he flew 3,000 miles from Nassau with the intention of doing only 25 yards of racing?

Hailwood found himself in the headlines in 1967, when Brands Hatch excluded him from the results of their Spring Bank Holiday meeting for riding his 250 and 500 cc Hondas instead of the 350 cc on which he had entered, even though the officials of the organising club had agreed his action before the meeting started. Mike again, it seemed, was unfortunate to find himself unwittingly in the middle of a dispute.

As the decade ran out, with Mike suffering financially because of Honda's pull-out from racing, Hailwood's retirement was anticipated. The official announcement came in 1969 and with it outspoken comments on his reasons. He said he realised that he could not, as a professional, afford to compete for little reward. He said he only wanted to ride in championship events, but there were no competitive machines left to ride. He said his decision had been forced on him by the state of racing as it then existed and by what he described as the FIM's antiquated set-up.

Both on and off the track Mike Hailwood had been responsible for some of the biggest bangs and most sparkling fireworks in a pulsating era of speed, drama and dispute. As he departed the scene everyone sensed that the curtain had dropped on an epoch.

# 8

# Hartle Loses in the End

Some riders give the impression of being immortal. John Hartle never did. Whenever John rode I was anxious for his safety, nervous until he had once again appeared back into the paddock. Not that John was in any way an inadequate rider. Far from it. He had a polished style and although courageous never seemed to take ridiculous risks. But his background of serious crashes during a distinguished career which was bedevilled by ill-fortune did not breed the greatest confidence.

It was at Scarborough in 1954 that he made his big-time debut. It was at Scarborough 14 years later, that his career was ended, and we were left to pay homage to a great racing motor cyclist.

Olivers Mount at Scarborough was never all that dangerous. Hartle's fatal crash there once more demonstrated the wafer-thin division between life and death when you race motor cycles. After a poor start, he had made up ground and, with typical Hartle determination, had set the fastest lap at 66.94 mph. He negotiated Mere hairpin, then accelerated up the steep climb. He could see John Blanchard ahead, Blanchard, struggling to get second gear, de-cellerated just as Hartle was beginning to fly. In the split-second in which decisions have to be made in racing, John decided the only chance of avoiding Blanchard was to try to move through on the left. The two riders collided. Both came off. Blanchard was all right. John crashed into a footbridge scaffolding at Quarry Hill and died.

Until the time of his death John Hartle had demonstrated an astonishing capacity for survival. He came through some of the most terrible crashes, refused to be intimidated by very serious injuries. Coming back after a premature retirement through injury, the future looked bright. But the bad luck which had

The incredible Derek Minter during that amazing Honda TT victory of 1962

Racing stars of the 'sixties at the 1967 French Grand Prix at Clermont-Ferrand. Ivy leads Read and Hailwood

Down goes Phil Read and the Yamaha, while Mike Hailwood and the Honda go round on the outside

Courageous John Hartle shows magnificent style at Oulton Park in 1967

Star of the 'sixties; super-star of the 'seventies. John Cooper gets down to business on his 750 BSA

Fred Cooper and the astonishing Cyclotron during the heydays
of 1967

A closer view of Cooper's remarkable machine

dogged John almost since his career began, beat him in the end.
It was the definitive stroke of fate. John's dedication to motor
cycles made him a great rider. It is ironic that this same
dedication required him to make the ultimate sacrifice. With
his passing the era of the great riders of the 'sixties was
virtually over.

Thirty-four at the time of his death, John began competing
in trials when 17, having learned to ride motor bikes at school.
After competing at Scarborough in 1954 he captured attention
by holding the lead in the Senior Manx Grand Prix. A year
later an empty petrol tank robbed him of victory. The following
year he graduated to being a member of the Norton works
team. Later he had works rides on a regular basis for both MV
and Gilera.

Significantly, it was at Scarborough in 1961 that he crashed.
Injuries kept him out of racing for two years. The very next
year he crashed again, this time even more seriously at Imola.
He fractured his skull and was advised to retire, but Hartle
shrugged off serious injury. Two years later, with medical
approval, he returned to racing.

Hartle's career was filled with incident, drama and disaster.
It was while riding the MV that his machine caught fire during
the TT, and his spell with MV was altogether not very happy.
Two years after joining MV he left, in 1960, to race his own
Nortons. In 1960 he won the Ulster Grand Prix and, in 1963 on
a works Gilera, was second to Mike Hailwood in the Senior TT
after lapping at 105.56 mph.

Like Bob McIntyre, John Hartle was always closely associated
with the TT races. His first appearance on the Island was in
1955 riding a Norton. He came sixth in the Junior event and
13th in the Senior. He was close the next year with a third and
a second in the Junior and Senior TTs. He joined former team
mate John Surtees on an MV in 1957 and rode the Italian
bikes on the Island in 1958 and 1959. In 1958 he became the
second man to lap the Isle of Man at over 100 mph and
although he suffered three retirements in the TTs of 1958 and
'59, he rode second to Surtees in the Junior of '59. His outstanding record in 1960 on the MV gave him a second place in
the Senior and he won the Junior, ahead of Surtees and
McIntyre. Gilera-mounted, he was back contesting both the

Senior and Junior TTs in 1963, collecting a second place in each race.

Gilera retired from racing in 1957, but in 1963 former star Geoff Duke made the now well known arrangement with Gilera to see if he could break the five year monopoly of the 500 cc World Championship held by MV Agusta. Duke got permission to borrow the two machines he and Reg Armstrong had ridden successfully in 1957, and chose John Hartle and Derek Minter as his two riders.

On the Gilera John showed his form by lapping Monza consistently at around 116 mph. He was second to Minter in the Hutchinson 100 meeting and at Oulton Park, when Minter set a new lap record in the 500 cc event at 91.86 mph, Hartle on the other Gilera also beat the previous record to finish second.

It was with some reluctance that Hartle returned to motor cycle racing in 1967. Not that his fractured skull had frightened him. He had tried to break into car racing, spending a lot of money in the attempt, but although he had numerous offers and tests, nobody came up with anything definite. Rather than give up racing altogether, he decided to make a come-back in motor cycle racing.

After his prolonged lay-off John was well pleased with his form during these early come-back rides. He won at Oulton, came first in the Production TT, took the Mellano Trophy at the Hutchinson 100, and ended the season by riding his Matchless into second place in the 500 cc World Championship. It was an astonishing achievement. The year was marred only by an end-of-season crash at Mallory, in which he sustained a broken arm.

Next season he was back in the saddle, though in 1968 he crashed a lot and had a particularly dismal time in the Isle of Man. Prospects looked good as the TTs approached. John had been trying to negotiate an MV ride and when he arrived on the Island he received a cable from Count Agusta confirming terms. He was to have the three-cylinder MV for the 350 cc race and the choice of two 500 cc 4s for the Senior.

Hartle was delighted, though a little cautious at the prospect of being astride the powerful and quick MV again. Said John: 'I went out to feel my way round but had to get used to the speed at which things seemed to rush up on the MVs. It was

my first time on something really quick since 1963 when I rode
the Gileras. It is great to be on something with urge, real urge
I mean.' He said the MV handled a lot better than the 1963
Gilera – and he got 195 mph out of that! He acknowledged that
he was not yet riding as well as before his Mallory accident,
but on the TT circuit this wouldn't be quite such a handicap
and would be more than compensated for by his experience
and knowledge of the Isle of Man.

Great excitement and interest centred around the expected
battles in the 350 cc and 500 cc TTs between Hartle and his
MV team mate Agostini. Hartle on form, riding equal
machinery, was seen as a serious threat to Agostini and some
nail-biting moments were eagerly anticipated.

In the Production TT a year earlier John had piloted a 650
Triumph Bonneville at 97.87 mph, in spite of his long absence,
and the crowds were eager to see him in action again. But it
was the Production TT of 1968 which swung fortune back
against him. Turning it on a trifle too much at Windy Corner,
he couldn't control a lock-to-lock wobble and was thrown off.
To his dismay, he was pronounced unfit for the Junior event,
but just in time the doctors gave him an all clear on Thursday
evening for Friday's Senior race.

Now was John's chance. Again he was thwarted. Hartle takes
us through the experience: 'Naturally I was a bit apprehensive
and when I reached Braddan Bridge and the thing started
going into neutral every time I changed down, I became more
so. I was having a race with Griff Jenkins. I would rush past
on the straights and he would get back on braking as I tried
to sort out the neutral. It is more difficult with a four because
when they hit neutral the engine usually dies through no fly-
wheel effect. It got worse and so I decided to get back to the
start as quickly as I could to get things sorted out. As I
approached Cronk-ny-Mona I decided to cruise through in top
gear rather than go down and get in neutral again. Obviously
it was a mistake because the thing went into an uncontrollable
tank slapper and I had no power to get out as I was only doing
about 6,000 revs in sixth. It was so bad that the lock stops were
smashed off and just as I thought I had got out of it, the bike
had another go and this time it won. We skidded down the
road together and I was very thankful to be able to pick

myself up. Somebody picked the bike up and I walked towards Signpost a very shattered man.'

For a rider with such a history of crashes it was unnerving to be falling off again. It also eliminated John's hopes of regaining a regular works ride on the MV. He was on trial and well he knew it. To attract attention he would need to have beaten Agostini. That had been his aim. It was depressing and disheartening that he wasn't even able to make a race of it. He had only managed one lap before his crash in the 500 cc event. It is easy to be wise after the event and there were shouts that Hartle should not have competed in the Production event. It was too risky with the more important Junior and Senior races to follow on the MV. But, as already noted, the confirmation from MV did not come until he was on the Island and by that time he had already promised Triumph he would ride their machine in the Production TT.

Between crashes, John won a number of races and looked outstanding. It seemed, after all, that he could continue on what might easily become the most sensational come-back in the history of racing.

After his severe double crashes in the 1968 TT Hartle admitted: 'My first thought as I picked myself off the road on Friday was that I should go into immediate and permanent retirement. I was a bit shattered, to say the least. It was the most disappointing TT week I have ever had. But I am not retiring. Provided I am fit I will be going to the Dutch TT next week and I will race with the same confidence that I had before.'

But the indomitable spirit which enabled Hartle to shrug off the effects of serious injuries as if they were bouts of flu, enabled him to ignore any signs of impending tragedy. Hartle reckoned he knew where he had gone wrong in the TT, the mistakes which had resulted in his crashing, and he did not anticipate making the same mistakes again. Not more than three months later the end came, when John was claimed for good by his bogey track, Scarborough. It was typical of the man that in spite of everything he had endured, he continued to be optimistic and, at the time of his death, was planning to go racing on the continent the following year.

Everyone liked and admired John Hartle. Anything but

flamboyant, a modest individual, the only outstanding characteristic to peep through the Hartle personality was his deep rooted love of motor cycle racing. When he came back following his retirement it was great to see once again the famous white helmet with the Chapel-en-le-Frith Coat of Arms on the front. Already he had dominated the track with some impressive rides. Then came Scarborough and it was all over in a few seconds.

To note merely that Hartle never won the World Championship is to grossly understate his ability and status. But for machine breakdowns, crashes, and long spells on the sick list, the crown would undoubtedly have been his.

Humour sums up the courage of John Hartle. When he crashed twice in the Isle of Man somebody said he had chosen to fall off in two very funny places. Retorted John: 'For only £15 start money I wasn't going to do it in front of the grandstand.'

That's how we like to remember Hartle – the Great.

# 9
# The Glamour Game

Suddenly, in the 'sixties, bikes were in again. After being out-
moded, old hat, as old-fashioned as the last generation, they
were once again the fun thing. Once the novelty of racing
minis and belting old bangers had gone, the 'in' set looked
around for something new to do. Buying a bike and perching
a bird on the back was it. The rockers and the greasers had
pointed to the bike's potential. Gleaming in its high-powered
newness, or strangely unfamiliar with small wheels and long
front forks, the bike became a brand new adventure.

Quick to exploit the new scene was a crop of Hollywood
movies with a common approach: a free-living, fun-making
easy-sex-orientated, racing-chasing adventure based on the bike.

For the genuine fun-loving bike owner and the more traditional motor cycle race fan, many of the bike movies did nothing
but set their teeth on edge. The plots were thin, the dialogue
banal, the bike sequences not always authentic. Most were
based on a maurading gang on motor bikes, a kind of up-
dated Capone in jeans and leathers. They spotlighted the rest-
lessness of youth, set against the broad, wild expanse of road-
side cafes and national highways.

*The Wild One*, made in 1953, didn't get a showing certificate
in Britain until well into the 'sixties, by which time we were
being swamped by a tidal wave of bike films. Among them
were *Angels from Hell*, about a Vietnam veteran coming home
to take up the leadership of his bike gang, *Hells Angels* and
*Hells Belles*. Then came perhaps the two best known movies of
the bike kind – *Girl on a Motorcycle* and *Easy Rider*.

The former starred a Harley Davidson and, of course,
Marianne Faithful. Marianne's role was an inspired piece of
casting. Beautiful, exciting, sexy, she had not been shy in letting

86

her views on life infiltrate the mass media system, and Marianne on a motor bike, appropriately geared out in leather riding suit, was well worth anybody's second glance.

*Easy Rider* was a sharper assessment of the phenomenon, made in 1968 and highly successful.

In these films, and others similarly inspired, bikes fitted like a piece of a jig-saw into the standard pattern which also brought in the clear hints of easy-sex, speed, gangs, violence, laconic attitudes based on a live-for-the-moment philosophy. Most of them carried the old X Certificate. It was part of the packaged bike deal.

Always before, bikes had been a man's world. Girls were now an essential ingredient of the new bike game. They provided the short skirts and high boots, to be thrilled and excited by the noise and power of a blasting Harley and the rough-love treatment of their heroes up front.

It was basically an American phenomenon, superficially exiting at first, but later to become stale and boring.

Then in 1970 came something different . . . and the trend was welcomed. *Little Fauss and Big Halsy* featured a couple of real riders who concentrated on the race game, travelling all over America in search of racing fame. Great atmosphere in this one . . . and not a gang in sight!

While the bike films had exploited the phenomenon, choosing to fragment the overall scene and publicise only one section of it, there was plenty of evidence in the 'sixties that bikes had made outstanding advances on middle-of-the-road and traditional fronts. *She* magazine in Britain, demonstrating the impact among females of the new role of the bike, posed Derek Minter with models for fashion pictures and included Agostini in their 'Gorgeous Men' series. Actress Fenella Fielding did television commercials for BP, posing on a bike during the Scottish Six-day Trial, and Dave Degens was paid £80 a day for a week to risk his neck crashing a bike for an episode in *Danger Man*. At Shepperton Studios, Dave made a habit of falling off the bike in a spectacular way . . . for the benefit of the camera and the ardent followers of this outstandingly popular TV series.

Also bringing bikes more and more to girls' attention was the increasing number of established film stars who made no secret of their love of bikes. Certainly the most famous was Steve

McQueen, but there were others including Clint Eastwood, who took the part of Rowdy Yates in television's popular *Rawhide* series. Clint was pictured chatting to Norton Villiers' John McDermott at Brands Hatch before going for a test ride on a 750 cc Norton P11A he hoped to take back to America with him.

In England to make a film with Richard Burton, it was appropriate that the picture of Eastwood should show a girl in the background, for girls were very much an active part of this new generation of motor cycle enthusiasts. Not only did they identify closely with the entire scene, they rode pillion in a provocative, fearless way never attempted by previous generations, and there was also a swing to more girls piloting bikes themselves.

Jocelyn Aitken, a bike rider for five years, looked good when she won the British Motor Cyclists *Miss Federation* title for the second time in 1967. Jocelyn, a 24 year old factory worker, had travelled to the event at Woburn in Bedfordshire from her home in Southsea, Hampshire on her 1959 BSA Shooting Star... with her boyfriend on the pillion!

But celluloid hero Steve McQueen did more than anyone to push the motor cycle to the forefront of fashion in the 'sixties. This abrasive, rugged character, as courageous and tough in private life as the picture he presented on film, built up an enormous fan following among star-struck girls during the 'sixties. Hypnotised by his quiet toughness, they avidly followed his every move, clung to his every word. They read everything they could about him, thrilled to his passion for speed and his obsession for big, powerful motor bikes. He brought the bike to their attention in a thrilling, exciting way.

In McQueen's case, the image was real. He was a genuine bike fan, with hard experience behind and ahead of him. He competed in American National Championship races, and was in America's first ever team in the ISDA annual long distance rough riding contest set against the clock. A couple of crashes put an end to his interest in this particular contest.

An adventurer and a rebel, McQueen relishes his love of high-powered motor bikes. He had a Paul Dunstall Domiracer tested for him at Silverstone and was reported, in 1970, to have six extremely fast motor bikes garaged permanently at his

American home. Rocketing to fame in the film *Bullitt*, which became famous for the sensational car-chase sequence, McQueen likes to do his own motor cycle riding in films and is never happier when allowed to do so, though the studios for obvious reasons bar him from the most dangerous sequences. In the film *Great Escape* it was said he did a lot of his own bike riding in that dramatic race for the Swiss frontier.

Not slow to recognise the potential of the bike as an excitement and glamour symbol for girls, the publicists and promoters lost no time. Advertisements, following the pattern set by the bike films, acknowledged the girl's role in the scheme of things. They showed mini-skirted models lounging against the gleaming chrome of the latest 'big banger', suggesting, as they were now convinced the message should, that a lad who was man enough to tame the powerful ccs of the newest mount, would for that reason be the lad with the biggest appeal for the girls.

There was an element of reason in it, as the *Hell's Angels* movement had so dramatically demonstrated, and the increasing number of girls at road racing in Britain and elsewhere showed that more conventional girls too were attracted by the roar of a big Honda or the scream of a Yamaha, and by the new, globetrotting heroes who piloted them.

Motor cycle racing was never so exciting, stimulating and rich. With the Japanese investing huge sums in their bid for world supremacy, with exotic machinery on view, with riders backed by squads of mechanics and the top racers being paid huge sums of money, the sport had found a new level of professionalism, polish and glamour.

It was natural that girls should be attracted by it, be dazzled by it, should want to become part of it. A works rider was an exciting individual, and his 'here today and gone tomorrow' existence only added to the fascination. Girls in the paddock were no longer a strange sight. Girls clustered round a star rider's caravan were no longer the hot news they would have been in the 'thirties, or even 'fifties.

Girls, the track-side dollies apart, had a logical and commonsense role to play in the lives of the travelling Grand Prix circus of the 'sixties. These were the wives and steady girl friends of the riders, who cooked, washed and generally looked-after their men while they raced round the European circuits.

They organised the daily routine and added a feminine fresh-
ness to the noisy, mechanical scene, warming up engines, kissing
their heroes as they moved out of the paddock to the start
grid, and clocking times. They were openly sharing a man's
world as girls never before had been allowed to do, sharing
the dangers and the uncertainties as well as the intense excitement and thrills.

Men who live dangerously like to let off steam with a flourish
and the after-race parties which were all part of the travelling
circus of the 'sixties are well known among racing men. While
it was fashionable at the time to exaggerate, to build up the
image, there is no doubt that on occasions, post-race booze and
birds could lead to brawls and punch-ups. Escapades of the
most hilarious kind were recounted and written into the folklore
of the times, and while these incidents were perhaps exceptional
they were the stories that held the attention and stuck in the
memory.

It would have been incredible if such situations hadn't existed
for the top men of the Grand Prix were buccaneering, colourful
characters, young, with red blood in their veins. Their track-side
antics and displays of clowning before and after races were
all part of the public image they felt they needed to live up to,
a means of relaxing the tensions and dramas of life and death
at high speed. Bill Ivy's Beatle hairdo and Mike Hailwood's
trendy moustache were as essential to the swinging scene as
were the eyes-widening accounts of the post-race parties.

Probably the most famous of these has been told countless
times and is doubtless added to with every telling. But the
story goes that in the early 1960s in West Germany, the wildest
party of them all took place. Everybody was there, a massive
crowd of racers and people who were involved with them.
There were prize presentations to winners of races, accom-
panied by trumpet fanfares, and the boss of MZ, a factory
which had done well in the events, had a potted plant dropped
into his lap. It wasn't long before the potted plants which were
used as a pleasant decoration to the venue had their potential
as party projectiles discovered. Before long potted plants were
being hurled to and fro across the room. When the band
decided it was time to stop playing, the crowd wouldn't let
them. There was, apparently, plenty of booze, and everyone was

having a swinging time. The band decided to pack it in finally at about 2 a.m. when somebody stuffed a potted plant down a trombone!

Other equally famous stories are exchanged where well known riders end up in swimming pools and where fights and scuffles develop from innocent beginnings. Then there was the time a world champion was said to have been found hanging upside down in a tree, when Mike Hailwood unwittingly found himself in the middle of a punch-up, and numerous occasions when riders have squabbled with police, particularly in Italy. Parties have developed into brawls and ended up with riders being threatened with a night or two in jail.

There was even one occasion, so Dave Degens told me, when Bill Ivy found himself and his bed in a car park at breakfast time ... but that was more of a practical joke than the sequel to a wild party!

Letting off steam was all part of living the Grand Prix way, but it would be wrong to think that parties took place every night and always finished in chaos. The majority of them were harmless, normal affairs with a few bottles opened and race stories exchanged. And according to the circus, the wildest ones took place during the earlier part of the 'sixties. Later the pace of racing became so intense, the issues so much more important as schedules became tougher and the competition for team places grew fiercer, that racing round the world lost some of its boundless off-track energy and abandon and became a more serious business.

During the 'sixties racing motor cycles was glamorised in a way never known before. The dirty finger-nails, shabby leathers, tatty general image which for some reason the sport had never before been able to shed, had suddenly fallen away. These new globetrotters were twentieth century gladiators, shining and sleek in their seven guinea shirts and fashionably cut suits. Their wallets bulged. They raced hard and lived life with a dash and sophistication which girls found irresistible.

Girls were indispensable to the new image of the motor cycle superstar, and often the escapades with which many parties came to a riotus end, had developed from nothing more than an innocent display of showmanship for the benefit of the females present. It was all spontaneous fun and to many who were not sensitive to the demands imposed, almost childish in its innocence.

The gloss of those smooth, sophisticated days has now largely disappeared or has been replaced by a glamour and excitement of a different kind. The Grand Prix circus of the swinging 'sixties is no more. The men and machines who blazed that particular trail hauled themselves well clear of the hobo image under which motor cycles had laboured disadvantageously for so long in the modern world, and conferred upon themselves as a result the gratitude of racers and riders who were to follow.

The high speed racing and living, the films, the girls and the hectic parties were not in vain!

# 10
# Ban the Mini!

Owen Greenwood was probably the most controversial figure in motor cycle racing in the late 'sixties. He built a three-wheel racer based on the mini, which, while fashioned more like a racing car than a bike, broke no rules so was able to race alongside conventional outfits in normal sidecar events.

The mini's superiority was absolute. Its advantage over traditional chairs was obvious and showed up regularly in the results.

In the beginning no one worried or got mad. Even in the excitement of the 'sixties, it was a dramatic innovation. It added a fresh dimension to sidecar events. We were curious, interested, fascinated. It was unusual, something different for us to see and talk about. With Greenwood and his mini down to race, a good crowd was guaranteed.

Then almost before we realised it, the innocent mini, its critics would have us believe, had grown to be a monster and there seemed to be no means of controlling it.

*Ban the mini!* The shout was echoed with increasing frequency. But how? Why? Though the Auto-Cycle Union was concerned about the growing opposition to Owen's racer, especially when other sidecar riders began to condemn it as a potential danger as well as providing them with unfair competition, they knew that within the framework of the existing law there was little they could do. As Greenwood explained: 'Although the close coupled wheels at the back meant that technically it was a four-wheeler, conventional sidecar outfits had previously been produced incorporating a similar feature and they had been perfectly acceptable for normal sidecar events.'

Depending on how you judged the situation, you could say that Owen Greenwood was shrewd and enterprising to develop his mini racer, or that he simply found a loophole in the law and exploited it. What is indisputable, however, is that he breached no rule... and to this extent the ACU found the situation a little embarrassing. As anger rose against Greenwood, they were unavoidably drawn into the conflict and it was left to secretary Ken Shierson to make the ACUs position clear: 'We have no proposals to differentiate between sidecar and three-wheeler classes. As far as 1966 is concerned, Greenwood and his mini are in the clear.'

The argument, aired by the press who recognised a good story when they saw one, raged more fiercely, while in the midst of the row Greenwood remained placid and implacable.

In a decade of motor cycle racing which was to become famous for its dramas, Greenwood claimed much of the attention for three seasons. Towards the end he was indirectly and not unexpectedly subjected to increasing pressure from other sidecar aces. When he finally quit, in 1968, he maintained he did so not because the situation had become too hot for him, as some of his critics had privately suggested, but simply that the time had come, after over 25 years involvement in the sport, to devote more time to his own motor cycle business.

When Owen Greenwood wheeled out his mini racer for the first time he had a tradition of motor cycle racing behind him, having shown interest in virtually every branch of motor cycle sport, including speedway, and having successfully competed in earlier years in both solo and sidecar road racing events. His Triumph was the first British outfit home, in sixth place, in the 1959 TT and in 1960 he was lying third when he was stopped when a pin fell out of the gear change while in top gear. Three years later his Matchless finished in seventh position in the TT, for which he received a silver replica, and he also won a silver replica on an AJS in the Junior TT that year.

Yet nothing remotely matched the recognition he was to win with the mini. Powered by a BMC 1,071 cc engine, with chassis and bodywork, and incorporating a car-type steering wheel, the mini nonetheless provoked no immediate concern or anxiety. After all, there had been basically similar ideas in the past. Cyril Hale had competed with sidecars in his Morgan three-wheeler, and later Roy Ward, again with a Morgan, but neither was taken very seriously.

Greenwood, on the other hand, and once he began winning, was a different matter indeed. The mini was first seen at the opening meeting at Mallory Park in 1965, but it achieved little during that season. Owen worked steadily on its development for the whole of the summer and throughout the following winter and by 1966 it was virtually unbeatable.

The mini, accepted with an air of amusement while it was struggling to become competitive, was now a positive menace to other competitors and when Greenwood flashed passed the flag at Mallory Park to win the world's richest sidecar prize of £500 in the Race of the Year, there were boos to be heard behind the cheers. Winning with a good deal of power to spare, Owen's performance in the race gave him two race records and he bettered Chris Vincent's month-old course record by over a second, registering a devastating 85.56 mph.

Owen Greenwood's success at Mallory created uproar. Pip Harris's passenger Ray Campbell claimed the mini was potentially dangerous when driven at speed in close combat with normal combinations. He reportedly went on: 'It does not need a great deal of imagination to foresee the disastrous results when some of the more enterprising and couldn't-careless drivers start to have a go. This is going to be a danger, so organisers, kill the idea now, before sidecar racing becomes stock car racing.'

Greenwood refused to react. He was mopping up very satisfactorily in many events and his outstanding win at Mallory served only to heighten the controversy, for he had swept to victory against some of the toughest opposition in the world including world champion Fritz Scheidegger and Pip Harris on BMWs.

Six months later the battle was still being waged. This time the man in the vanguard of the campaign to outlaw the mini was top-line sidecar man Colin Seeley. Said Colin: 'I should like to see action taken now before the class becomes a complete shambles. Now is the time for the ACU to make a decision.' Colin made no secret that the mini, with its 4 wheels and 1,071 cc, 4-cylinder engine was so superior to normal outfits that it simply cleared off and left them all behind. His main

concern was that competitors coming into sidecar racing would
be tempted to build themselves a similar machine, which would
cost them a lot more than the normal outfit and would be
dangerous to other competitors.

In the heat of all the argument, Greenwood said little. He
continued to race his mini and win many of the races he contested. It became increasingly clear that, with the feeling which
was now developing against the mini, something had to happen.
Towards the end of the 1966 season it was strongly felt that
the Auto-Cycle Union would have to respond to growing
criticism and it was suggested by many observers that they
would adopt FIM rules which would make a ban possible without penalising large capacity sidecars. But the problem was
simply this: by limiting sidecar races to machines of 750 cc,
and thereby eliminating the 1,071 cc mini special, they would
of course bar genuine sidecars of over 750 cc, such as the 998
cc Vincent-powered outfit.

In the close season there was speculation that the major
short-circuit race organisations were working out a formula
to prevent the mini competing during 1967. The rumours
were well founded and at Brands Hatch and Mallory Park
a top capacity limit of 1,000 cc was imposed for sidecar events.
Thus the mini was automatically eliminated, though no such
limit was imposed at Cadwell Park.

Greenwood was not to be sidestepped easily. He fitted a
970 cc engine, carried out other modifications, and found his
mini once again eligible for open competition with the traditional chairs, even at Brands and Mallory.

The fight was on again, and continued right through until
Owen retired in 1968.

But why did he build it in the first place? Explaining the
circumstances which led to the development of the mini
racer, Greenwood told me in 1972: 'In the first instance my
reasons for wanting to build it were purely personal. I had
long wanted to build a competitive three-wheeler and had
spent some time over a period of years while racing
Triumphs, considering ways and means. However, the
Triumphs kept me busy so I had little or no time to get
down to anything practical concerning a three-wheeler.'

Owen explained how he had raced successfully with

Triumphs and began to look around to decide what he would
do next. He began again to think about the possibilities of a
three-wheeler.

'I became curious to know whether I was capable of building a three-wheeler which could beat the more conventional
racing outfits. That, basically, is why I finally got down to the
job. That and the fact that when I mentioned the idea around
from time to time, everyone said it just couldn't be done. Being
the kind of man I am, this made me more determined than
ever because this is the kind of challenge I like.'

Owen got his head down, chalked out the plans on his workshop floor one evening early in October and by working even-
ings only, he and his race mechanic Roger Campton had it
completely built by January.

The mini's weight, ready to go, was 620 lb., brake horse
power approximately 85. Its wheelbase was 6 in. shorter than a
conventional mini, its track some 6 in. wider. Drum brakes at
the front were used for the first season, disc front brakes for the
second and third seasons.

Such was the mini's superiority that in three seasons it
brought Greenwood more than 60 victories, 2 British Cham-
pionships, the Brands Hatch Championship, and lap records at
Mallory Park, Brands Hatch, Snetterton, Cadwell Park, Croft,
Silloth and Kirkistown. He also established British and World
Speed Records at Elvington.

Owen was never really happy once he had to drop the mini
down to lower power. 'It wasn't really competitive and I didn't
have the time to give to the further development work it
needed.' About its advantages when powered by the big engine,
Greenwood maintained that it wasn't that much faster than
conventional outfits on the straights, though it would reach
110 mph on the fast Park straight at Cadwell! 'Where we did
score was on acceleration out of corners and the mini would
*drive* round corners while a normal outfit drifts, soaking up the
power,' he said.

Owen is adamant. 'I never did abandon the mini idea,' he
insists. 'Three years is a long time for me to keep anything,
even something as successful as the mini, and the only reason I
did not race again was that I had to devote more time to my
business. I had, after all, been involved in the sport for a very

D

long time – over 25 years in fact – when I parted company with
the mini.'

He dismisses as ridiculous the view as I heard it expressed
at the time that he was virtually hounded from the track by
the growth of public opinion against his mini.

'Absurd' he retorted. 'As a matter of fact, all the time I raced
the mini no pressure was put on me by anyone from the ACU
or any other organisation to stop racing it. The mini, after
all, had been built to comply with the regulations.'

Owen went on: 'The first rider to see the mini felt sorry for
me . . . for being so wrong. When the adverse reports began to
appear in the press I was all the more determined to prove I
could win. Other riders too seemed to consider the whole thing
a bit of a joke at first, until I started to win, though among
spectators at meetings there always seemed to be as many for
the mini as against it. It created great interest and stirred
people into thinking about new outfits.

'With Roger Campton, who was my friend as well as race
mechanic, and Terry Fairbrother, my passenger who supported
me so magnificently, the mini helped us to make many new
friends. It was all great fun and I really would like to do it all
over again.'

Early in 1968 Greenwood bade farewell to the mini. For
£650 he sold it with both engines to Bill Copson and Ken
Allen, partners in a motor cycle business in Ashton-under-Lyne.
About the mini reputation, Copson was reported as saying at
the time that he didn't care what was said about his driving of
the mini, he wouldn't be breaking any rules and he wanted to
win races.

The mini certainly gave him a great opportunity to do just
that and at its first outing with its new owner, it charged to
another controversial victory in the 8-lap sidecar final at Cadwell
Park.

Eighteen months after Greenwood sold the mini to Copson
and Allen, it was sold again, this time to 19-year-old farmer and
motor cycle racer Andy Chapman of Leeds. Complete with the
two power units, the mini cost Chapman £675, but very soon
after starting to race it, prize money had reclaimed £250 of his
investment.

Said Andy: 'I had a fair bit of success with it and raced it for about a couple of years. But I was having trouble with it and was having difficulty getting parts as they needed to be replaced. When the thing blew up half way through the season at Cadwell I decided to let it go. I sold it to a chap called Graham Little who said he would use it for sprinting.'

In December 1970, the basic controversy continued to rage. This time Greenwood was taking no part in the battle which centred around trikes or three-wheelers, though the issues were the same. *Motor Cycle* ran a poll among its readers, who came out strongly in favour of an outright ban. Typical of readers comments was a letter from Bob Irvine of Cardiff. Bob put it this way: 'I have no wish to see cars racing, whether they have three wheels or four. If the three-wheel monstrosities are to race, let them race each other, but not at bike meetings.'

Even the Competitions Committee of the ACU finally saw fit to take action. They decided to segregate three wheelers and sidecars, but this decision was reversed by the General Council in 1971, leaving the issue a domestic matter for individual organisers whether they wish to have events for three wheelers and sidecars combined.

Shortly after selling the mini Owen Greenwood started work on a more conventional outfit, though unusual by normal standards. He was signed with Castrol at the time who were linked with Honda and Owen wanted a small Honda car engine to power the new unit.

Honda in Japan seemed interested, but nothing came of it. Owen, undeterred, continued with the project. The new outfit was extremely low, with mini wheels, centre hub steering and had a very light chassis. Built round a Triumph 650 unit construction crankcase, special consideration was given to brakes. Said Owen: 'You must have good brakes. Too many drivers rely on the drift of three wheels to provide braking. We got the outfit finished and even tested. It went well, but expanding business responsibilities left little time for any thing else. After it had been hanging around the workshop cluttering up the place I got rid of it. So far as I know it never did race.'

Greenwood told me that for 15 years he had thought about his mini and when he had it completed it was the realisation of a dream. Still passionately fond of motor cycle sport, Owen Greenwood has taken to trials riding and, according to his wife, loves it and continues as ever to talk long and often about motor cycle racing.

Time has softened the fierce attitudes which identified the dispute over Greenwood and his mini. Retrospectively, the wrangle seems less important. The fire has gone. Yet at the time, in the heat of the moment and midst uncompromising postures, Owen Greenwood piloted the mini racer to a succession of exciting victories and earned them both a permanent place in motor cycle history.

# 11

# The Big Boys of the Circus

Looking back on the early days of his career, Phil Read was once reported as saying: 'I think I was probably quite a big-headed little swine really.'

It is the kind of outspoken, no-nonsense comment we have come to expect from Phil, one of the greatest riders of his generation. Big-headed or not is open to debate, but one thing is certain: Phil was never short of grasping the opportunities that came along. In the mid-'sixties I went to Brands Hatch one Sunday with a photographer friend, Cy Stork. The object was to take new shots of Derek Minter in action. Phil was there with his gleaming E-type. We took a picture and I later sent him the print. Phil wrote back thanking me . . . but he took greater pains to point out that the car was for sale and did I want to buy it?

It is this kind of opportunism, coupled of course with his outstanding skill on the two-stroke, which rocketed Phil Read to the top of the international league. With Mike Hailwood, Jim Redman, Bill Ivy, and Giacomo Agostini, he became a giant in the Grand Prix circus of the 'sixties.

He once put the inspiration of Geoff Duke and John Surtees battling at Silverstone as the reason for his entry into motor cycle racing. His first victory came at Castle Combe in 1957, but it wasn't until the end of 1958 that he started to make significant progress. In 1960 he registered a double victory at the clubmans races at Oulton Park and won the Senior Manx Grand Prix.

A Luton lad, he was born in 1939, but he outgrew his tentative beginnings to race Yamahas round the world as a high-salaried works rider and to develop a successful Yamaha boat agency in the Channel Isles. His first TT success came in 1961 when he won the Junior on a Norton. The following year he took fourth position in the 500 cc world championship, Mike Hailwood securing the title with Alan Shepherd and John Hartle second and third.

Read was coming good at just the right time. He had piloted a Gilera in 1962 and when Yamaha invited him to saddle a 250 twin in Japan the big chance had arrived. By now motor cycle racing was buzzing with big names and the Japanese involvement was pumping the sport full of new life. Hailwood had secured the 500 cc world title with his mighty MV, but in all other classes except sidecars, Japan was supreme with Ernst Degner, Luigi Taveri and the remarkable Jim Redman.

Phil was rushing to cash in on the big time, to be part of the new scene. His trip to Japan and the Yamaha debut could bring him what he wanted. He rode well, finished third behind Redman and the Japanese rider Ito, and was offered a Yamaha contract, their first to go to a European rider.

During the remainder of the 'sixties Phil Read and Yamaha were synonymous. Throughout the great and historic battles he fought with Redman in '64, during his power-packed performances to take the world championship for a second time in 1965 and the 125/250 cc double world championship in '68, in the squabbles with team-mate Ivy and even after Yamaha had retired from the racing scene, Read rode Yamaha to become the most loyal and enduring warrior of them all.

Knowledgeable, shrewd, courageous and talented, Phil Read is perceptive and outspoken. He gained a reputation as a rebel and added his share of colour and controversy to the sensational 'sixties.

Phil's first world title came in 1964 on the Yamaha and he looked set to gain a second three years later following a keenly fought 250 cc Grand Prix series with Mike Hailwood. The final race of the series was in Japan. It would decide the championship, but both Phil and Mike retired to tie with 50 points each. For a while it was uncertain who had secured the title. Hailwood had five wins against Phil's four, but Phil had a second place in one event while Mike's next best was a third place.

The odds seemed to favour Read and press reports even announced him as the winner, but he was to be disappointed. After quite a tangle during which the FIM seemed as confused as everyone else, Hailwood was given the decision. The FIM ruling gave the number of *wins* and not the number of *points* as counting to a world championship. Mike had more wins, Phil had more points. He admitted his bitter disappointment and his fans said he'd been cheated.

Phil Read's racing career started quietly enough, but his outstanding rides against Jim Redman during 1964 which wrested the 250 cc world title from the tall Rhodesian picked him out as a rider of immense stature. Read was a handsome Hell Raiser with a princely style and a fast-developing character on and off the track. Against some of the most dynamic, forceful and colourful personalities the motor cycle race game had known, Read found a place, and constantly made news with his strong convictions, uncompromising actions and, let it not be forgotten, his sensational success with Yamaha.

It was Read in 1968 dominating the scene with one sensation after another. In March he flew to Rimini, but the Italians wouldn't allow him to compete.

By July that same year, Phil was dubbed 'The Rebel' because of his refusal to let team-mate Bill Ivy take the 250 cc world championship. Phil said he would quit the Yamaha team rather than deliberately take second place in the three remaining 250 cc classic events. The Read-Ivy feud had begun. It was also in '68 that Read hitched himself to the Weslake world-beater project.

Phil's double world championship was won in 1968. Even though his name was absent from the lists the following year, his position as a personality in world racing was strengthened. With the golden days of Honda ending, Redman retired and Hailwood only occasionally astride bikes, Phil had a clearer field and dominated the scene. Bill Ivy, challengingly colourful and explosive, was to die that summer.

In January 1969 Read's interest in the developing Weslake project, which aimed to put a British 500 cc twin world beater on the track, continued to excite interest. It was Phil a month later, dominant and punchy, announcing, according to *Motor Cycle News*: 'I'll win four TTs.'

The biggest news of all came in October when Phil announced he was pulling out of the Weslake scheme. Big news because the former world champion had drastically curtailed his racing during 1969 in order to work on the project, to help develop and market complete machines. They had orginally been planned to be available by the previous June, but the Weslake's appearance in Ireland's North-West 200, with Read riding, suffered lubrication problems in practice and didn't even complete a lap. Further difficulties prolonged the delays and with Phil tempted by new season offers, he chose to go back to full-time racing for 1970. Two Grand Prix wins in Italy in September 1969 brought him invitations from major Italian organisers to contest their big-money, early-season events. Phil, hungry again for a full racing season, decided to abandon the Weslake project.

In 1970 Read dominated the racing scene. In March it was Read being rushed unconscious to hospital after crashing in the 350 cc event at Rimini and, later that month, it was Read defying doctors orders by discharging himself from an Italian hospital. In May it was Read angrily snubbing MZ after the East German factory had approached him at the end of the previous season because, it was alleged, of a disputed agreement for him to test their machines in Italy. It was Read in August racing to a dramatic sub-second victory over Charlie Sanby and John Cooper in the Hutchinson 100, Read again in September clashing with officials at Cadwell Park and walking out without riding because of a row over practice, and Read still further in October making a fuss about £330 medical expenses which he said were due to him by the organisers of the Cervia meeting in July.

A year later Phil Read returned to championship honours by taking the 250 cc world title for 1971, making him a world champion five times.

Back in 1968 Phil Read had already achieved immortality in motor cycle racing. With four world championships to his credit he admitted to having thoughts of retirement, but he said he intended to ride for at least one more year. In 1972 Phil Read was still one of the biggest draws in the business and while the road racing scene had changed significantly since the sizzling 'sixties, was still pulling on his leathers and dashing to success all over the world.

It was against big Jim Redman that Read fought some of his most illustrious battles, especially in 1964 when Phil, refusing to be intimidated by the daunting prospect of giant Jim, already the possessor of four world titles, rode relentlessly to take the 250 cc title from the Rhodesian.

Redman rode with immense distinction, without flourish, as a true professional who never travelled faster than he needed to win. Not for Jim speed for speed and glory's sake. Winning was the object. To win by the biggest possible margin didn't impress him. He raced intelligently and was sensible enough to realise the value of a Honda team place and made sure he kept it.

Jim was born in Britain, but went to Rhodesia in 1952. He developed an interest in motor cycle racing and when he met John Love, then moving from bikes to take up car racing, the two became friends. Jim helped John with car preparations and in return John allowed Jim to have a race on his Grand Prix Triumph. At this stage Redman was so much of a novice that he had to borrow John's racing leathers before he could take part, but he finished in seventh position and an outstanding career had begun.

Already a big star in Rhodesia, Jim set his sights on Britain. He did well, but was not the sensation he had hoped to be. In 1959 he returned to Rhodesia, disappointed, and announced his retirement.

Redman, who had experienced his share of hard times, had fixed his mind on a works contract. For him the uncertainty of struggling to survive through financial privation offered no attraction, yet he found the art and exhilaration of racing motor bikes more thrilling than anything else in the world.

He decided to try once again and returned to England in 1960. He hoped for a works contract with MZ, but an opportunity occurred when Tom Phillis was injured and Honda looked around for a replacement. Jim eagerly took over at short notice and at Assen, in the Dutch TT, finished 7th in the 250 cc event and 4th in the 125 cc race. When Honda planned to make an outright assault on motor cycle road racing they remembered Redman's performances in Holland and invited him to join them as a member of their works team.

What Jim Redman had worked for was now his. He became captain of an immensely powerful Honda team and rode brilliantly to capture his share of world honours – 250 cc world champion in '62 and '63, and four-times 350 cc world champion in four years, '62 to '65 inclusive, all on Honda.

His six world championships brought him a fortune . . . and a coveted MBE. Less blatant than some of his contemporaries, Jim nonetheless didn't conceal that he was in racing for the money and would scheme and argue for what he felt he was worth. It was a disagreement over expenses, I believe, that kept him from the United States Grand Prix at the beginning of '64, the season which quickly became famous for the intense rivalry between Redman and Read.

The situation was explosive from the start. Redman was an established champion, Read one of the most exciting, ambitious, talented young-men-in-a-hurry around at that time. Read was after Redman's title and everyone knew it. Honda looked invincible, but Yamaha had improved their machines beyond recognition and were determined to surprise the world.

The epic duels which followed were contested all over Europe and throughout a sensational season. The gauntlet had been thrown down, accepted, and Redman and Read were left to battle it out. 'Racing like this is magnificent for spectators,' said Redman later, 'but it's torture for riders. You know you daren't let up for a split second or the chance to win is lost. I was convinced I was going to end the season a nervous wreck and I know Phil felt pretty much the same way.'

It is fair to say that Jim had never been pushed so hard before, and the intensity of it all must have been hard even for a seasoned hell raiser like Redman. Phil, of course, saw the season for what it was: a magnificent opportunity for him to move in permanently among the top riders in the world.

Though both riders contested the Spanish Grand Prix, Provini on his Italian Benelli outrode them to win, with Jim in second place and Phil third. So it was at Clermont-Ferrand in France that the first clash materialised and gave promise of what was to come. For more than half the race they were closely contested, but mechanical failure eliminated Redman just when it looked as though he might be inching ahead. Read went on to win.

It was at the Dutch TT as Assen that the sparks really began to fly and in a day of near delirium resulting from some of the most sensational racing ever seen, Redman manfully wrenched victories from Read in both the 125 and 250 cc events.

Jim's own vivid description in his book *Wheels of Fortune* captures the guts, vigour, skill and intensity of it all. Writes Jim: 'For mile after weary mile we raced in each other's shadow, heeling so far over that our fairings scraped on the corners, screwing our aching eyes against the sun, and troubled every inch of the way by each other's determination to win. The corners were murderous because of the rubber and the old smears of oil that had leaked from other machines in previous races. The speeds were breakneck. And we were "accidentally" knocking each other's legs at speeds of around 130 mph as we braked side by side into corners and struggled to snatch the initiative.'

This was demon action all right, a realisation of the saga of sensational dicing which had been promised at Clermont-Ferrand. Phil described the same race like this: 'The Dutch was another ding-dong, and there was never more than a couple of bike lengths between us in the 250. We were swopping the lead all the way, and went over the line almost locked together – with Jim inching home by about a wheel.'

Physically and psychologically, the strains and pressures were clearly prodigious, but for the ultimate victor there would be enormous reward. Phil said later: 'There was a big bonus at stake for me as Yamaha reckoned a world championship victory would boost their prestige and, therefore, their sale of machines.'

These were indeed stirring times and the magnificence of Jim Redman at Assen in 1964 comes through only with an objective look at what he achieved: in intense heat, lap and race records were shattered in the 250 cc event and he and Read lapped everyone in the race except Tommy Robb, while in the 125 Redman collected a lap record and, together with Read, established such a scorching pace that the first six men home outpaced the previous lap record set only a year earlier! In the 350 cc event Jim was two minutes better than Mike Hailwood, again setting up new lap and race records. In the one day he won three major races against high-flying opposition and was now ahead of Phil Read in the hotly contested 250 category.

In Belgium, Redman led Read by 10 points, but Phil pulled back some of the ground in West Germany and even more in

East Germany when our two heroes had to contend with Mike Hailwood, piloting a particularly fast MZ. Mike was leading when he fell off, leaving Phil and Jim, both a lap ahead of the remainder of the field, to battle it out. Phil took the honours.

At the Ulster Grand Prix, in driving rain, Read once again outpaced Redman to win by a minute, so at Monza Jim was in a desperate situation. He needed victory at Monza and in Japan in the final round of the series to retain the title. Read had only to win at Monza and the title was his.

But now, into battle came a powerful new enemy for Phil Read, a gleaming, six-cylinder 250 Honda capable of 17,000 revs. The Honda backroom boys had been working furiously to prepare the machine for Monza. keeping Redman's secret weapon disguised and under covers. Read somehow got wind of it and was stunned. It was a nasty blow to Read's confidence and gave Redman a huge psychological advantage as the bikes were wheeled out ready for the start.

For Redman, the Monza dream was never fulfilled. On the new, mighty Honda, he stormed ahead of Read at the start, but soon it was obvious that all was far from well. The engine was overheating and Jim couldn't get the pace he needed from it. By the half way stage Phil had come up alongside. Soon he roared ahead to take the race at a record 113.91 mph.

One of the most momentous battles of all time was over. Phil Read had snatched the title from Jim Redman and in so doing had given himself his first win in the Italian Grand Prix and brought Yamaha their first world title.

The Japanese race was only a formality but Redman, his new powerful six having been sent back to the factory immediately following the Italian Grand Prix – he always maintained it hadn't been ready at Monza, well out-powered Phil's Yamaha.

Though he had yielded the 250 cc world crown to Phil, Redman secured the 350 cc championship for the third year running, winning every race, a remarkable achievement.

He was to win it yet again the following year, after which Mike Hailwood carried on to bring the 350 title twice more to Honda, before the field was left clear for Agostini and the MV.

If ever there was a golden boy of the bike world it was Mike Hailwood. Being born with a silver spoon in your mouth takes a lot of living down and Mike, in spite of a sensational, shatteringly successful career which brought him 12 TT victories, 9 world championships, and the widely accepted tag of the greatest racer of all time, never completely succeeded.

Perhaps it was a vain hope that he ever might, for no achievement, however great or enduring, is enough for some people to square the natural advantages they felt Mike enjoyed. In America it would have been different. Whether Mike's father was a millionaire or a tramp wouldn't matter. It was up to everyone to grab what chance they had.

In Britain though, with the most charitable attitudes going to the underdogs of sport, provoking Mike became the 'in' thing.

His father Stan Hailwood said that Mike had to pay his own way, but there were many who found it hard to believe. Did it really matter? Was it not irrelevant clap-trap? Hailwood did more than enough to prove himself as an all-time great of motor cycling.

He was showing good promise at seventeen and at 18 competed in four solo classes of the TT, registering a third place, 7th 12th, and 13th. His progress was phenomenal – three out of four ACU road racing stars at eighteen, a works rider two years later, two TT victories and a world championship in 1961.

. Hailwood's spectacular career had begun. He rode a wide variety of machines at British short circuits but began to dominate the world and annihilate almost all opposition only when he mounted the fabulous MV and contested the 500 cc class.

Born in 1940, Mike originates from Oxford where his father, a millionaire, was once head of Kings of Oxford, the motor cycle dealers. Young Mike was undoubtedly helped by a father who took a keen interest in his son's love of motor cycles, organised the arrangements behind the riding, generally encouraged him to do well, and knew the value of showmanship. Yet the need to earn and make racing pay, the driving force behind the ambitions of so many young riders, was never the urge which Mike could call on when the going got tough, the setbacks just a little too cruel. He had to be a self-starter all the time.

Amazingly versatile in the earlier days of his career, Mike first appeared in the TT honours list in 1958 when he secured third place in the 250 cc class riding an NSU. Another third, this time in the Senior class, was his in 1960 when he rode Norton behind the powerful MVs of John Surtees and John Hartle.

In 1961 Mike still rode Norton in the 500 cc class, but was astride a privately-entered Honda in 250 and 125 events. In the Isle of Man that year he won all three classes, adding the 250 cc world title later in the year.

It was in 1962 that Hailwood signed for the MV factory. His career rocketed. Taking over from such distinguished riders as John Surtees and Gary Hocking, Mike dominated the 500 cc class for the next four years. Few rider-factory relationships are totally harmonious and Mike had his moments with Count Agusta, bureaucratic boss of the big MV concern. In 1962 the 350 MVs were already outpaced by the Hondas, which Jim Redman was riding so brilliantly, and over in Italy local lad Giacomo Agostini was claiming the attention of MV as a promising young rider. No one was entirely surprised therefore when Hailwood, tempted by what was reputed to be the biggest cash offer ever made by a motor cycle factory to a racer and after four years with MV and obviously ready for a change, switched to Honda.

The battle of the heavies which riveted our attention for two thrilling, sensational seasons was on.

Following his invincibility aboard the MV, much was expected now of Mike on the mighty Honda. Without diluting his obvious achievements, it must be said that during his MV years, Mike had faced little opposition. His races had become mere processions, with Hailwood and the MV far ahead of the field, and his victories predictable. With Mike now aboard a challenging Honda, the pace under pressure and the reliability of the MV could be decisive.

Mike again was oustandingly impressive. His dazzling successes swept aside all opposition in the 250 and 350 cc classes, and he gained world titles in both categories in 1966 and '67. But with the bigger Hondas, Mike failed where he so much wanted to succeed. Agostini, the handsome Italian, had taken over from Mike as number one MV pilot. He was good and courageous and his machine was more reliable than the Honda turned out to be. Ago took the world title in '66 and again in

'67 and, with Honda's interest fading and Mike being tempted by soundings from the car racing world, went on to win the title for the remainder of the 'sixties. With Mike's Honda challenge spent, however, the 500 cc class lost much of its interest. With virtually no serious opposition, Ago's succession of victories became boringly predictable.

Against a galaxy of competing talent, in the sizzling, effervescent days of the 'sixties, Mike Hailwood became the acknowledged King. He was in the vanguard of a new breed of motor cycle racers, the globe-trotting glamour boys who rode their heart out against the exciting background of big-money contracts, exotic machinery and the glory of the Grand Prix.

Mike smashed countless records and made history almost every time he climbed aboard. His contribution to motor cycling is legendary and immeasurable. When he handed over his crown it was to a similar character, for Agostini too comes from a highly prosperous family intensely proud of its offspring.

Agostini perpetuated the glamour image set by the swashbuckling heroes of the 'sixties. His film star looks, broken English accent, carefree smiling personality and moneyed background made him instant box office and pure magic for the thousands of British fans on the look-out for a new hero.

Devastatingly conscientious in the saddle, Ago has a flippant off-track ease born of the independence which comes from escaping the drudge of having to earn your own living. Of his early working life when he drifted into his father's flourishing transport and road-building business, he freely admits: 'My heart wasn't in it. If I wanted a day off I took it and as I got more and more interested in racing I took more and more time off until I stopped working for him completely.'

Unlike Hailwood's father who, as a former racing star himself appreciated Mike's obsession with bikes and encouraged him in his ambitions, Agostini's parents were anxious about their son's interest in motor cycle sport. He had owned a scooter at 9 and at 15 was competing in local trials. His first serious road race was on a Morini in 1963 and although mechanical trouble forced his early retirement, Ago had demonstrated sufficient style and dash to capture the Morini factory's interest. The very next season he was offered a regular works ride and that same year outpaced the skilful and established Provini to take the 250 cc Italian championship. He signed for MV in 1965 and his performances catapulted him from near obscurity to world class within nine months. He missed by a hair the 350 cc world title, mechanical failure in Japan putting it out of his reach, and he was runner-up to Hailwood, his MV team-mate, in the 500 cc class.

When Hailwood switched to Honda the magnificent duels, fought out in the highest sporting traditions yet unyielding, boundless, titanic affairs, brought sensation and spectacle to the Grand Prix racing scene. In that first season Agostini secured the world title in the final 500 cc round in his own country, at Monza. He had already scooped the 350 cc TT and towards the end of the season, before excited crowds in Britain, won Mallory's 1,000 guineas prize and also collected 350 and 500 cc victories at Brands Hatch in the Race of the South events. Such was his impact on world motor cycle racing, and to such a degree had he raced into the hearts of the British race-going public, that he was voted Man of the Year in the poll organised each year by *Motor Cycle News*.

Within a couple of years Ago became everybody's darling. He was friendly, sensible, modest and very much respected. He was a dashing new hero who rode fearlessly and although only 5 ft. 5 in. tall could handle the big MV with commanding ease. Devastatingly handsome, he had all the glamour trappings to compel fan worship. He was successful, moneyed, unattached, gay, with a smile which flashed easily and made girls' knees turn to jelly. When not riding he would ski, swim, go to parties. His potential as a film star was soon spotted and he made three films in Italy. He was said to have three sports cars, a luxury boat and an income within sight of £35,000 a year. His fractured English added to his appeal, as did his expanding business interests. Girls scrambled for a touch of his smooth racing leathers and among the 100 fan letters a week were pleas for snippets of his hair and clothing.

Agostini was born close to Bergamo in June 1943. His first competitive win on a motor cycle was in 1962 when hill climbing in Italy on a 175 cc Morini. The following year he entered his first road race Grand Prix when trouble with his 250 cc Morini forced him to retire. In 1965, competing at the Nurburg-

A leaping getaway by Agostini, hotly pursued by Cooper (3) and Nixon (5)

Gary Nixon on the 750 Triumph. The new-style Bell helmet
puts Gary almost out of view

The style of the great Bob McIntyre at Silverstone

Before the fireworks begin. At Brands Hatch in October, 1971,
Cooper, Agostini and Nixon prepare to fight it out

As we remember gentleman Fritz – Scheidegger on the incredibly reliable BMW outfit in the 1966 TT

The handsome film-star looks of
Giacomo Agostini – debonair
man-about-town and speed
champion

Ago blasts round Mallory Park on the sensational 500 MV3

ring on the 350 MV, he secured his first Grand Prix victory. By 1970 he had collected eight world titles. More were confidently predicted. His home town greeted him as a hero, waited impatiently for his periodic returns from any one of a score of countries. In 1969 Ago delighted his British fans when he announced he would foresake competition in the two last Grands Prix of the season in favour of a round of British international events at Oulton Park, Cadwell Park, Mallory and Brands Hatch. They liked heroes who were close at hand.

Neat, clean, said to be a non-smoker and non-drinker, Ago continued to be a credit to bike racing, projecting very much the boy-next-door image with his easy charm and friendly approach. He kept himself out of the squabbles and frictions of the 'sixties, avoided being drawn into rash statements against other riders and organisers, and was by no means a controversial figure. His contract with MV was generous, even by Agostini's standards, and he always fully valued it. Any serious disagreements he might have had with the Count were kept secret. He acknowledged that Count Agusta was paying out the money and had every right to call the tune. About a possible visit to England he said: 'I hope to come again next year, but that will be up to the organisers ... and Count Agusta.' On another occasion he said: 'There is no question of me deciding to go and ride in a race simply because I want to. I must first ask MV and only when they agree can I make my entry.'

Such attitudes were almost old fashioned in the challenging, abrasive days of the 'sixties, as was the close relationship he continued to feel for his family, in spite of all his success.

Hailwood, Agostini's prime protaganist in the MV-Honda battles, went on to race cars. Ago, too, received tempting offers, one from Ferrari, but in the early '70s Giacomo Agostini was still essentially a bike personality, one of the big boys of a travelling circus which had largely disappeared since the pulsating, throbbing days when he first made his name.

These then were the glamour boys of the travelling speed circus – Hailwood, Agostini, Ivy, Read, Redman – who flipped from circuit to circuit, this country to that, with more ease than most of us find when going for a day out at the seaside. Motor cycling's hobo image had gone. These were glossy characters caught up in the gigantic bubble of an artificial world which

burst when the Japanese factories called it a day. But while it
was good, it was very good indeed.

The pace was hot, rewards exceptional, living was today and
now. There was room at the top for only a few, and the
Hailwoods and the Ivys were envied by a legion of big-time
also-rans convinced that they could prove themselves as brave
and talented if only they were given the chance.

Although in terms of public recognition and acclaim the
acknowledged few made most of the news and were caught up
in the biggest dramas, other riders found a firm place in the
Grand Prix scene, riders like Ralph Bryans, Stuart Graham,
Hugh Anderson, Hans Georg Anscheidt, Dave Simmonds and
Luigi Taveri.

Bryans concentrated on the small classes, gaining the world
50 cc championship in 1965. An Irishman, he had earlier concentrated on home events, winning the Cookstown 100 and
finishing in third place in the North West 200. His big break
came in 1963 when, following test rides for Bultaco, he signed
a contract with them. Almost at the same time Jim Redman,
scouting for Honda talent, had been impressed with Ralph's
riding. Two months after Bultaco's offer came the chance of a
works contract with Honda. It was a more attractive offer and
Bryans signed, Bultaco sportingly withdrawing their offer after
realising that Bryans, financially, could make only one choice.

In his first year with Honda he won four Grands Prix and
came second to Hugh Anderson in the world championship –
an impressive performance. This was a remarkable achievement
when you consider that the only circuits he knew at all at the
start of the season were the TT and the Ulster. He secured the
50 cc world championship for Honda the very next year.

Hugh Anderson came all the way from New Zealand to gain
fame in Europe and take no fewer than four world championships. His double success came in 1963 when he secured both
the 50 cc and 125 cc world titles for Suzuki. In the smaller class
he had captured the title the previous year, but was to lose it to
Ralph Bryans on the more competitive Honda the next year.
In the 125 cc class it was honours in alternate years for Luigi
Taveri on a Honda and Anderson on the Suzuki, starting with
Taveri in 1962 and ending with Taveri in 1966.

Hugh, so the story goes, had started riding round the family farm in New Zealand when he was 10. He had a go at scrambling before invading the European scene in 1961. His achievement in securing the 125 cc world title in 1965 was perhaps the most impressive. At the Nürburgring he set up new race and lap records on his way to an outstanding victory. He was unbeatable again in the Spanish and French Grands Prix, the latter event again bringing him a new lap record at a speed of 94.41 mph. He set a new lap record on the Isle of Man, though was unplaced in the race, and could only reach a disappointing third in the Dutch. More disappointment in East Germany, Czechoslovakia and Ireland, but he finished the season in devastating form, winning the Italian, Finnish and Japanese Grands Prix, to take the World Championship.

Though all gained works contracts, Taveri, Graham, Anscheidt and Simmonds never achieved the public recognition in Britain of Bryans and Anderson – Taveri, perhaps, because he was an Italian, Anscheidt because he was German, but both rode to many distinctions. On Suzuki machinery, Anscheidt captured the 50 cc world title for three years running from 1966, while Taveri raced to world 125 cc championships in 1962, 1964 and 1966. Simmons, on a Kawasaki, secured the 125 cc World Championship in 1969.

Stuart Graham, son of Les Graham who was killed riding an MV in the 1953 TT, was signed to a works contract with Suzuki in 1967 after a number of promising outings on a Honda had been ignored by the Japanese factory, but he didn't win a world title during the 'sixties.

Kel Carruthers was another character of the 'sixties who claimed a section of the stage of the Grand Prix circus. He gained a world title in the 250 cc category on a Benelli in 1969.

The Grand Prix roundabout at its most flamboyant was an unreal fantasy world created out of the Japanese factories obsession for world racing domination. It was created almost overnight in the scientific laboratory atmosphere of specialised, exotic machines, and it disappeared almost as quickly. It was a phenomenon particular to the 1960s and although its excesses largely disappeared when Honda and Yamaha withdrew, it had a lasting influence well into the 'seventies, but in a far less lavish, much more subdued form.

# 12

# The Fast Ones from America

The Americans can be boastful and brash, but they know how to sell themselves and recognise a commercial opportunity when they see it. Britain takes pride in underselling itself, while in America the hard sell has become a way of life. Internationally their attitude can create enemies and set up resentment, but it gets them talked about, which is more than half the battle when you live by public attention.

It was in the 'sixties that American motor bike stars and their tough-line views on racing first became widely known to race fans in Britain. Gritty character Bart Markel reportedly said: 'Racing's a business. It's not a sport. Not to me anyway. I am there for the money.'

Gutsy stuff this, to a British sporting public which had cut its teeth on amateurism and doing the thing for fun. Equally alien to the British fan was another remark attributed to Markel: 'Nice guys don't win. I ain't a nice guy.' Even in a rapidly changing Britain, we still found it hard to swallow such a large dollop of candid comment in one go. Just a little shocked, we watched while Bart indulged himself in his bad-guy image. It was the cut and thrust of the big business jungle brought down to the race-track level.

On the other hand you don't win American racing titles by being tentative and indecisive. You don't win honours by specialising. You must be a great all-rounder to gain recognition. The idea is to pile up as many points as possible in a grinding series of varied events including half-mile and mile dirt-track racing, road races, speedway and what the Americans call TT races, which is a dirt-track with artificial jumps. Markel proved he was no slouch and won the title three times. His comments riveted attention. *Cycle Magazine,* in the United States, called

him Jack the Ripper of the dead half miles, the closest thing
to a real Jack the Ripper ever seen in American motor cycle
racing.

Markel, it seemed, had no time for trophies. 'I'd rather have
the money or something useful,' he was quoted as saying. It
was flamboyant, brash, and, to the English view, typically
American. It was all rather slick and very much a novelty to a
home bred public fed on British short circuit racing and the
traditional world classes events. Even the enclosed helmets and
stripey leathers all seemed part of the showmanship of motor
cycle racing in America, and Markel was a great showman.

Born in Flint, Michigan, he was scramble riding at twelve
and within a year of turning professional was spotted by Harley
Davidson as a potential champion. They sponsored him, but he
crashed the machine at Daytona on his first ride, and didn't
think he'd be given another chance. They just gave him another
machine and this remarkable character became one of their
super-stars.

The all-American-boy image, clean shaven, close-cropped hair,
a toothpast smile and sunglasses – they were all central to the
modern bike hero of America racing. While Markel was not
cast perfectly in this mould, Gary Nixon came much closer to it
as America's No. 1 racing idol.

Gary, from Oklahoma, played the showmanship game even
down to the Christian name emblazoned on his white stripey
leathers. At twenty-six, described by *Motor Cycle Racing* as
'currently the hottest property in American racing', Nixon was
scintillatingly extravagant with a single-minded approach to the
racing business. He was Grand National Champion in 1967
after a season of cliff-hanger situations which kept American
fans speculating right to the end. At Daytona the same year he
raced to two major triumphs in two days – winning for Yamaha
the 100-mile lightweight race and then securing the 200-mile
race on a Triumph against heavy Harley-Davidson competition.

Nixon was there in 1968 when 32,000 people, the largest
crowd at the time ever to attend a motor cycle race in the
United States, were drawn to the famous Astrodome in
Houston, Texas, and saw brilliant riding by Nixon and other
American professionals including Cal Rayborn, Chuck Jones,
Mert Lawwill and Bart Markel. Gary hurtled, slid and flung his

machine round the circuit, and was supreme on the day.

In more traditional Britain the showmanship antics of the American riders, both on and off the track, were observed with mild amusement. There was also a feeling that the American courses, which included many more flat-out straights that made racing there more of a monumental burn-up or extended track racing rather than anything else, were by no means so demanding on the riders. We found it hard to think that the American aces could ride with much success on the British short circuits. The Americans were brave enough, they could go fast, but their type of racing required more than anything else a machine that could gallop. Riding skill wasn't so important. Put Nixon in a race against our own stars on British circuits and we would see what happened.

For years a technical hitch prevented such a possibility happening. Two representative bodies exist for motor cycle racing in the United States. It is unfortunate that the one with the greatest representation is not affiliated to the National Federation of which the British Auto-Cycle Union is affiliated. But eventually, what British fans had waited so long to see, did happen. Nixon came to Britain, and at first he found the going hard. Phil Read wrote after Nixon had competed in the Race of the Year at Mallory Park in 1970: 'What a deep end to throw the Americans into. They were swooped-under, out-braked, and leaned-on, and all in all during the first 10 laps were given a bad time by our national aces. However, I feel Gary Nixon especially came through with flying colours. I hope Nixon and Du Hamel do not think they were being victimised in any way. This type of hard riding with no quarter given is usual during such a big race and the Mallory Park circuit is, in my opinion, the most demanding as far as race riding ability goes. Power and speed are not the most important factors. Certainly the tracks in the States do not demand this standard of high speed cornering ability of both rider and machine. Daytona, for example, which is recognised as the top race in the United States, is over 2 miles of flatout riding round the bowl and the infield there is only one riding corner taken at about 90 mph.'

Many feel that British racing could learn much from the American example, particularly in the sophisticated techniques of the 'hard sell' of an event. Crowds attending motor cycle events in America are small compared with the enormous throngs at the major races in Britain and particularly on the continent, but the Americans don't bother too much about dragging spectators to the event. The money comes from selling it to television, radio and the cinema. And bike manufacturers are not slow to appreciate the sales pitch of such an exercise, for the screening of an event brings motor cycles and the successful machines before an enormous number of potential bike buyers.

The appearance at British tracks of American aces and of British stars at Daytona adds an excitement and thrill to racing on both sides of the Atlantic. It brings a new dimension when new opposition is seen and some of these American riders are sensational characters with a great ability to bring in the crowds.

The most palpably extraordinary character, though not strictly a traditional motor cycle racer any longer, but who came to the attention of the British fans in the 'sixties, is the amazing motor cycle stuntman Evel Knievel. He started on bikes at 10 years old, decided later he wanted to make a lot of money fast, so packed in racing and put an act together which, for in-depth daring and showmanship, has no equal. Dare-devil Evel makes a fortune by making enormous leaps astride his Harley-Davidson. He can pack 99,000 people into the vast Astrodome in Texas. Just one performance can bring him as much as 40,000 dollars. *Cycle World* reported: 'Strong men turn white and women scream when Evel starts up the ramp.'

Evel has a permanent limp. He collected it when he attempted a record 50 yards leap. He didn't quite make it, lost control and crashed into a brick wall which gave him brain concussion, a fractured hip and pelvis, and various incidental injuries. A chunk of metal now connects his leg bone to his hip bone, causing the limp.

Knievel is the complete showman. He lives the part. He will tell you his tractor-trailer which takes all the paraphernalia of his act, including six motor cycles and tons of steel ramps, is the longest vehicle of its kind in the world and cost him 140,000 dollars. It's air-conditioned and incorporates a lounge, office, dressing room, television and stereo.

He appreciates the tension and drama in his act and is only too happy to share this with his audience – at a price. He's been described as a cross between a circus act, a ballistic missile and a rodeo. He cheats death, makes money from doing so and spends it with total relish.

Knievel is said to make about ten jumps a year, taking flight over rows of cars parked side to side – as many as 19 on one personal record-breaking occasion, and is paid at least £10,000 a show.

An exceptional character by the most extreme standards, Evel Knievel has an even greater ambition. He wants to leap the Grand Canyon. The authorities smiled when he mentioned it to them, then went on with their work. But Knievel wasn't joking. He immediately invested a great deal of money in having a special machine designed.

It was in 1966 that he applied to the Department of the Interior for permission to jump his jet-powered motor cycle over the Grand Canyon. He was turned down, so he offered 100,000 dollars in an attempt to try and swing the deal. Again it was turned down, so, it was reported in America, he bought some 300 acres of Snake River Canyon near Twin Falls, Idaho, about 1,000 ft. deep and ¾ mile across. Knievel planned to make the monumental jump in the 1970s in his special rocket powered projectile called a sky cycle.

It's difficult to know how much of what Evel says to believe, so outrageous and astonishing are his statements. He's stumbled across a goldmine of a gimmick and, smoothly attired in beautiful white leathers and (off track) walking around with the aid of his gold-topped cane, his showmanship is impeccable. A feature film about this dare-devil motor cycle stuntman was seen in London for the first time in the late summer of 1972.

But that 'Grand Canyon' – type leap, is that for real? No matter how much ballyhoo Evel may generate, only when he actually takes off will we know for certain.

# 13

# Racing Ban for Dave Degens

Dave Degens had everything going for him as a short-circuit road racer in the mid-'sixties, but an act of folly brought a shock end to his promising career. Found guilty of receiving stolen engines, he was sent to gaol for six months. The Auto-Cycle Union took away his licence. By the time they gave it back to him it was too late. He was done with short circuit rides, though he made a spirited and successful revival in a display of defiance in long distance road races, mainly abroad.

Degens' race suspension caused a storm of protest and the ACU was fiercely criticised for unusually harsh and unfair teatment to a well known and respected rider. John Cooper, Dave Croxford and others campaigned vigorously on Dave's behalf, organising a petition in his support. Their plea was that Degens, then doing time, was already being punished and as Cooper wrote: 'Surely in British justice you have to pay only once.'

The ACU were unyielding. It was left to Degens, later, to initiate proceedings which brought him a personal hearing when his indefinite suspension was changed to a period of two years.

Four years later Degens talked frankly and without embarrassment about the incident which wrecked his racing career. 'I was pretty choked at the time,' he told me. 'I felt I'd been victimised, made an example of. The ACU ban cut me up far more than going to prison, but you get over these things.'

The career which was to end so sensationally really began in 1959. 'I didn't particularly want to race at first,' recalls Dave. 'There were about half a dozen of us who just drove around on the road. The father of one of us bought his lad a racing bike and he reckoned he was going to be world champ. This needled some of the other lads who were out to take the 'world

champ' down a peg or two. They persuaded me to have a go
to show him what riding was all about and I entered a non-
expert event at Thruxton.'

Dave came off. He didn't have a very good start, but was
doing well when, coming through the chicane, he caught the
back wheel of the bike in front. But he'd seen enough of racing
to know he wanted to go again. At Thruxton the next year he
won on a Gold Star. Degens was on the way.

He did more racing on the Gold Star and then bought an
AJS 7R from Geoff Monty. He raced on this for a year and did
well enough to show a profit on the deal when he sold it for
£25. 'I think I entered thirty or so races and all I had to do was
fit an oversized main bearing,' remembers Dave.

Then, in 1961, came the first of a series of enforced inter-
ruptions to his promising career. It wasn't injury or shortage of
cash, but National Service which claimed him! He had to go
into the Army, though as a soldier he maintained his interest
in bikes and towards the end of his conscription Geoff Monty
sponsored him in one or two events.

Once out of the army he raced more regularly and began to
get noticed. He attracted a string of sponsors during his career
including Sid Lawton for four years, Paul Dunstall and Steve
Lancefield for a year; and Tom Arter loaned him bikes.

A tie-up with Triumph main agent Sid Lawton brought Dave
outstanding successes in both 1965 and '66 when he won the
500 mile race on a Triumph Bonneville prepared by Sid, and
the Barcelona race on a Dresda Triton.

Such was Dave's reputation at this stage that he had already
qualified as a candidate for a works ride with Honda. A year
before, Honda team rider Alan Shepherd, who had come off and
damaged his back in Japan, suggested Degens as his replacement for the TT, should he not be fit again by then.

A Honda works contract was the most powerful thing that
could happen to a racer and there would have been plenty of
scrapping for Alan's place, had it been generally known that
there was a vacancy. Dave's try-out on the Honda at Oulton
Park, therefore, was kept secret, but Dave said later that on his
second lap on the 250 Honda he equalled the 500 cc lap record.
'Then,' said Degens, 'Alan had me go round timing the race,
knocking four seconds off, then two seconds off, riding to orders

really. I did this quite easily. I just sliced 200 revs off and it worked out, and they were very pleased with it.'

When the TT came, though, Dave didn't get the Honda ride. There wasn't a bike available for him, as the one he should have ridden and been smashed up at the French GP a few days before.

During this period Dave was recognised as one of the bright and rising stars, certainly one of the top half dozen short circuit racers in Britain. In long distance events too he was making a name. In 1965 he and Rex Butcher went to Montjuich, Barcelona, and registered the first all-British win in this famous 24 hour event on the Dresda Triton and Dave, with Barry Lawton this time, won the Thruxton 500 miler on a works Bonneville. He won with Butcher again in 1966 in the British Marathon at Brands Hatch. In 1966 one writer predicted: 'He will almost certainly be signed by a works team before the end of 1966.'

Degens, for all his skill and racing success, was not a track fanatic. 'I never set myself any specific ambitions, but I enjoyed my rides and the wins I had.'

Motor bikes, rather than just racing, was what he asked of life and three years earlier, with an eye to a business career, he had bought a share in Dresda Autos, near London's Putney Bridge. At that time the business was at Hampton and was dealing mainly in scooters, but with Dave's influence resulting from his passion for motor cycles, business in bikes was developed with Dave building and marketing the Dresda-Triton machine which he rode with success around 1964–65. In 1966 and '67 Degens was a familiar and popular figure at most of the home short circuits. His stocky frame sat well on a bike and his cheerful personality won him many friends. In Gloucester-shire, riding an Aer Macchi, he secured both the 250 and 350 cc events and riding his 650 Dresda Metisse was first in the 1,000 cc 8 lap race. It was an impressive performance.

Said Degens recently: 'I was winning enough races not to worry too much about the business – it was simply a way of investing in the future so that when my racing days were over I could concentrate on building up a business of my own.'

An abrupt end to his bright future on the race track was

nearer than Dave knew for within two years he found himself
in the middle of the kind of scandal motor cycle racing had not
experienced before.

It was an ironic twist of fate which led to the conviction and
then the racing ban, for it developed from his own outstanding
success on the track with his own Triton machine. This created
a lot of business at Dresda Autos and the firm were faced with
a growing need for Triumph engines. This led to painful con-
sequences for Dave.

Once the dust had settled little was said. When Dave Degens
came back to pick up the pieces of his racing career and a
business which had nearly died on him, he wasn't the hot news
he had been when he had been branded a 'bad boy'. But four
years later he spoke to me frankly and with remarkable
candour about the events which led to his gaol sentence and
racing suspension. Dave and I had worked together earlier on
my *Book of Motor Cycle Racing*, before the events took place
which were to shatter his career. But comfortably seated in his
smart Hounslow home not far from London Airport, I wanted
his side of a story which had been by far the biggest sensation
of all in a sensational period for motor cycle racing.

'*What really happened Dave?*' I asked.

He thought for a moment, then began: 'I suppose it goes
back to the time I rode a works BMW in the 24 hour race in
1964. I took a lot of notice about things which were letting
riders down on bikes and in my mind I built up the sort of
bike which I felt would overcome these problems, a bike which
I felt would win. This sort of thing... Geoff Dodkin was two
pits away from me and he was going through primary chains,
so I thought about using duplex or triplex chains. Compression
was another problem. I thought about using a low compression,
while still getting the power from having large carbs and high-
lift cams. I put these and other modifications into my Triton
bike and in 1965 went back to the 24-hour and won it with
Rex Butcher.

'The Triton was Triumph-based and because of this win, I
got lots of publicity and lots of lads wanting a similar bike.
This meant I needed a lot of Triumph engines. My business
soared and I went from employing one to employing four in a
very short time. We were buying engines where we could and

the word soon got around that we needed engines. A chap I'd bought from before – all he was doing was buying and selling engines – said he had five engines available and was I interested. I told him I was and he sent them over. At the time I was paying between £90 and £100 for an engine, so I said I'd take the five from him at £75 each.

The deal was agreed. I paid a cash deposit there and then, and let him have a cheque for the balance once I'd received the engines. So far as I was concerned that was the end of it.'

*What happened then?*

'I was at the garage as usual four or five days later when I was swooped on by C10, the police branch which deals with stolen bikes and cars and such like. They went right through the place and of course came across the engines. Then off they went. They came back, told me they had reason to suspect they had been stolen. They chased it all through and the trail went right back to the factory, but they didn't believe I didn't know they had been stolen.'

In court, some time later, Degens pleaded guilty to receiving engines stolen from Triumph's Meriden factory. 'I thought I'd get a fine,' Dave told me, 'but bang, mind the doors, and that was it. I was shattered. Six months in gaol.'

He served four months, the first six weeks at Wormwood Scrubs and the remainder of the time at an open prison near Aylesbury. Racing was suspended, his business was in jeopardy and coming up with the darkest and heaviest cloud of all was the Auto-Cycle Union, who suspended him *sine die* (without naming a day). He was subsequently granted a personal hearing and the period of suspension determined. This meant it would be almost a year after he came out of prison before he would be allowed on a race bike again.

There was uproar in the sport. Many riders and fans condemned the ACU action.

Certainly it was a tough reaction on the ACUs part, without precedent it seemed in the entire history of that organisation. Of no help to Degens' case was the fact that other riders were involved at the same time, which perhaps suggested to the ACU that strong measures *had* to be taken to demonstrate to riders generally the risks they would run if tempted into similar circumstances.

There is no doubt that the ACU were empowered to act as they did. Degens had committed an offence under the breach of the Union's prejudicial conduct competition rule. While the ACU wouldn't be drawn into giving further reasons for their action, there is little doubt that they were concerned about the public image of motor cycle racing, had no action been taken against the riders. While Cooper, Croxford and others came out with strong attacks on the ACU, *Motor Cycle News* in an editorial put forward a sympathetic view: 'Motor Cycling has not in general a good name in the eyes of the majority of the public. Its image can only deteriorate further if these men are allowed again to preach on TV, win races, or become the idol of youngsters. The ACU decision must have been taken to protect the image of motor cycling and even to enhance it in the public's eye. What they have said, in effect, is that no man shall be entitled to profit further from the sport he has dishonoured.'

Dave Degens went to gaol in November 1967. His suspension was announced, then a 90-minute private hearing of Degens appeal by an ACU Court resulted in Dave being able to regain his licence in March 1970.

Dave Degens was a hell-raiser of outstanding merit with plenty of courage and a fine style on a bike. Professionally, the timing and circumstances of events didn't work in his favour. Poised for the big time before the ban, it was impossible for him to reclaim his former status when he returned. The big-money opportunities had departed with the disappearance of the Japanese factories, the fire had gone out of his ambition, he was disinclined to take to the short circuits again.

Said Degens: 'I wanted like hell to get back into racing because the ACU had said I couldn't. I fought for the freedom to do just that. Then, once I could, I began to wonder if it was worth it. My motor cycle business, which had been brought to its knees because the finance company had pulled out, was flourishing again and, because I was needled with the ACU and would do hardly any meetings in England because of that, I lost the atmosphere – and its the atmosphere of racing more than anything else which keeps you going.'

I asked Dave to tell me about the reaction within the sport to everything. 'Marvellous,' he said. 'Blokes in the race game know what its all about. You live fast, die fast, spend fast. You put a lot into it and there's no easy way. They felt I was unlucky and said so. When I got my licence back I was chuffed at the way offers for rides came in. At some circuits I was offered almost twice the start money I had been getting before the ban.'

But Dave's first job was to get his business moving again. It had almost collapsed during his absence. It was the sort of business which depended very much on his personal contribution – for instance it was he who made the contacts for the supply of parts; it was he who had the influence to encourage and develop sales; it was he who supplied the basic drive and energy. Deprived of these essentials Dave's wife Donna had a hard job keeping things going. A friend provided a £500 loan. Using each pound like a bar of solid gold, £500 was never made to go further, small amounts being allocated over a wide field in order to keep everybody reasonably happy. Part-payments were made wherever possible to conserve the meagre capital.

There were staff problems, but somehow the business was kept going. The transformation on Dave's return was miraculous. He recalls: 'I remember the very first week back at work. We took £1,000. It was just as if everyone had been waiting for me to come back. It was a tremendous thing for me. My real friends were still around, but the hangers-on had gone. I was left with good solid people who stayed with me. I put a lot of effort into the business and trade just increased. I didn't have so much time for racing and it wasn't so important any more.'

Degens also found, in spite of the good offers made to him to return to the short circuit scene, that a lot of the money had gone from the game. In 1966 he'd been approaching the Minter and Ivy level, commanding almost as much start money, but the general money levels two years later were not so impressive. 'Derek would confirm this, for it was one reason why he retired when he did,' explained Degens. 'On the other hand, I certainly had the urge to race again. I felt I must.'

So Dave Degens made his comeback, but not strictly as a road racer. He concentrated on long distance events. Nor did he stay for long. It was more like proving to himself that, despite the injustices to which he reckoned he had been subjected, he could still ride a motor bike and win. He won the Scarborough Gold Cup in 1969 – it was on TV over all England – and he took the famous Barcelona 24-hour race along with Ian Goddard in 1970, when both were virtually retired from regular riding. For Degens it was his second victory at Barcelona, the first being five years earlier in happier days when he shared the honours with Rex Butcher. In between had been the unhappy experience of the conviction, gaol sentence, and racing suspension, but it was a successful Degens, tired and hot in the Mediterranean sun who, in 1970, became the only Briton to win the Barcelona marathon twice on a British machine.

In 1965 it had been a Triumph-based twin which had taken him to victory. In 1970 he rode one of his own Dresda models which, significantly, housed a Triumph twin engine. The bike was finished only a week before Dave and Goddard rushed off to Spain.

A year earlier, with Dave making an impact on the racing scene once again, he and Goddard might have won. They led for seven long hours, but a couple of broken chains and other malfunctions held them back at the end to take sixth position.

It was during his success in the 1970 Barcelona race that Degens started thinking he'd had enough racing. Said Dave: 'We were 20 laps, that's about forty minutes, in the lead, so I wasn't exactly killing myself. I was going round slowly, having already done eighteen hours and some six hours still to go. I wasn't really enjoying it, I didn't need the money because the business was going like a bomb again, and I wasn't really getting any excitement from it. At the end I told my wife: 'I didn't enjoy that at all.' She said if that was the case it was probably time I packed it in. I thought about what she'd said ... and decided to call it a day.'

Every race career has its share of hazards. Dave Degens' suffered more than most. He was unlucky that he was just old enough to be included in one of the last batches of conscripts so that he spent a couple of years as an infantryman when he could, and should, have been gaining wider experience and sharpening his technique racing round Brands Hatch and Oulton Park. In his enthusiasm to build up a business he took risks, got caught and paid the penalty, unusually stiff by many peoples reckoning. The ACU took away his licence. Finally his wife left him and took their daughter with her.

In spite of it all a lot of enthusiasm for the race game comes through when you talk to Dave Degens. He talks fluently, with the confidence and style typical of the Londoner, about the 'sixties when he became a fallen star. He still bristles when you mention the ACU, but he is not remorseful or self-pitying about what happened.

Of course he tries to square the record, as he sees it, going over the old ground, trying to remember dates and situations.

About the Honda works ride, Dave insists that a lot of people had the wrong idea when he missed the TT because the bike he should have ridden had been pranged on the Continent. 'They thought I'd lost my chance of very glossy prospects with Honda but I had already made up my mind to turn the offer down anyway. My business at the time was going well. I was making good money racing as an individual, because I had little expense. With Honda I could have doubled my income, but the outgoings would have been enormous. In the proposed deal, I was to get a fat contract fee and keep all I could win, but out of it all I had to pay for the transport of bikes, mechanics and so on, and take out other expenses. Of course I was chuffed and dead keen at first, but then I got to looking at it differently. It I took a works ride and started to ride full-time as a professional, Dresda Autos would have had to be sold so that my real income might not have been that much higher. My wife and daughter would have to stay at home while I was skulling round Europe. At best I could last four years, and then I'd have to set up in business all over again, building up from scratch. I'd probably come out of it all with very little money because the life you lead on that sort of high-speed circuit means you spend it as you get it.

'I reckoned the deal just wasn't on and I'm sure now that I did the right thing. A year later Honda tempted Hailwood away from MV. With Mike in the team do you think they would have kept me on?'

Dave smiled as he thought about it, as he did when I asked him about racing today. No, he didn't think the standard of riding had improved, but bikes were now much faster. 'I can remember when you could draw a blanket over the first five

E

in a race. You'd be fighting like hell. On two or three occasions at Brands I can remember going round the hairpin – I used to take a funny short line there right round the inside – and looking across and actually having Derek Minter touching my fairing and Paddy Driver touching Derek's fairing. It's not really dangerous because you're all going the same speed. It looks sensational, but it's like going round holding hands really. Now they all follow round in procession and its the fastest bike that wins.'

Dave says its easy money these days. 'I told one of the blokes that I reckoned racing was a bit of a pushover now and that I thought it was about time I came back. "Don't you dare," he said, "We don't want you to spoil it for us".'

Degens keeps well in touch with the race game through his business, supplying special parts and modified frames to many customers on the Continent as well as in Britain. 'I haven't been to one race this year,' he admitted, 'but I know what's going on. I had Barry Sheene in to see me last week and I spoke to Phil Read on the phone today. Rodney Gould, Barry Sheene and the Finnish bloke (Jarno Saarinen*) alluse my swinging arm on their Yamahas and Japauto has just won the Bol D'or with a Dresda.'

Dave Degens is a good salesman and he keeps very busy. The sensations of the 'sixties don't come to the surface very often. 'It's happened, over and I like to forget it,' he said. For an hour or so we relived vividly, with the help of memories, press cuttings, and photographs, the incident that stunned motor cycle racing and momentarily stopped it in full flight. Then I was gone . . . and Dave went back to business, selling bikes, not racing them.

---

\* Saavinen has since been killed, along with Renzo Pasolini, in a tragic accident in the 1973 Italian Grand Prix at Monza.

# 14

# Those Honda Years

Honda's commitment to Grand Prix racing was the driving force of motor cycling in the 'sixties. It spanned nine years; brought them eighteen world championships and approaching 140 classic victories. Commercially, it secured them a leading position in the sale of motor bikes throughout the world, from which they were to continue to benefit long after their resignation from the racing circus.

The Honda story began tentatively enough in 1959 when they went to the Isle of Man to compete in the 125 cc TT. Their six-speed twins were much admired as beautiful examples of engineering, but ridden in the main by Japanese jockeys, they weren't good enough to take top honours. Provini on an MV, Taveri on an MZ and Hailwood on a Ducati occupied the first three places, though Honda secured the team prize, their machines finishing in sixth, seventh, eighth and eleventh positions.

In 1960 Honda applied more steam to their attack. Facing the disappointment that their home riders were not really good enough for world competition, they engaged Australians Tom Phillis and Bob Brown and it was during 1960 that Jim Redman, who was to make fame with and for Honda, had his first ride on the Japanese machine. They now attacked on two fronts, competing in the 125 and 250 cc events on the Isle of Man and at a number of continental classics. There were clear signs of the outstanding success which was to come and Redman ended the season in fourth place in the 250 cc world championship.

There is no doubt that in 1961 Honda saw the opportunity of a major breakthrough and in preparation signed Luigi Taveri to support Redman and Phillis. Brown had been killed during 1960. Bikes were also given to Mike Hailwood and Bob

131

McIntyre, and with MVs virtually retired from racing, the field for Honda was clearer. The effort was worthwhile. Tom Phillis became 125 cc world champion and Mike Hailwood 250 cc world champion. There were also impressive displays in the TT, with Hailwood winning both categories.

More concentration and more money was applied to securing Honda's place in world racing during the 1962 season and it produced plenty of incident and drama. They collected three world titles. The season began with beautifully-prepared bikes in the 50, 125, 250 and 350 events and with popular Tommy Robb added to the team. The early season 350 cc entries were enlarged 250s and it was later in the season that Redman rode the first full 350 Honda. Fortunes were mixed in the Isle of Man during 1962. Tom Phillis was killed in the Junior event. Taveri won the 125 cc TT, but the big sensation on the Island was the remarkable victory of Derek Minter on the non-works Honda in the 250 cc. Derek outpaced Jim Redman on this occasion, but Redman brought *official* honour to Honda with world championship crowns in both the 250 and 350 cc classes. Taveri was invincible and took the 125 cc title.

Honda had won outstanding success and world-wide fame, but at what price? The cost was enormous. What would happen for the new season? Which way would Honda go? For a year they stopped to catch their breath and put some money back into the bank. In 1963 they decided to pull out of the 50 cc championship and their 125 cc machines couldn't match the speed of the Suzuki, but Redman romped away to bring them yet again both the 250 and 350 cc world crowns.

In 1964 Honda took up the challenge once more, investing heavily in racing with a new four-cylinder machine for the 125 cc events and, later in the season, a six-cylinder racer for the 250 cc world championship. But the competition was hotting up and Redman was faced with an insistent Phil Read on a Yamaha. Phil took the 250 cc world crown from Jim, though Redman's outstanding success in the 350 cc event continued and he was again declared world champion. Taveri brought Honda their second world championship during 1964, securing the 125 cc crown.

There were mixed fortunes again for the giant Japanese factory in 1965. Once again they seemed to be at the crossroads. Having signed on Ralph Bryans in 1963, Honda re-entered the 50 cc world championship and with a new twin-cylinder machine Ralph won his way through to secure the world title. In other categories it was a different story. In the 125 cc events, the Honda couldn't match the speed of the Suzuki ridden by Hugh Anderson, who went on to take the title, and they had no answer to the exhilarating performances of Phil Read and the Yamaha in the 250 cc category. It was left to Redman, once again, to bring them their second world title of the year, in the 350 category.

In both riders and machines Honda now faced the obvious need for re-establishment and they set about the task with resolution and an extra-bulging purse. They signed Mike Hailwood and developed some exciting new machinery. It produced outstanding results and in 1966 they raced to three world championships and gained all five solo manufacturers world titles. In the individual categories a complete Honda run-through was thwarted by Hans-George Anscheidt on a Suzuki in the 50 cc class, Giacomo Agostini in the 500 cc class, and Luigi Taveri in the 125 cc category. Hailwood was brilliant and rode to 250 cc and 350 cc world titles. Redman, who had done so much to rocket Honda to world domination, broke an arm during 1966 and decided to retire. He had brought Honda world victories in 1962 and '63 (250 cc) and in the 350 cc class had raced through uninterrupted from 1962 to 1965.

At the end of 1966 Honda's brilliant reign was ending. But on the basis of pure results the 1967 season was again to be impressive. They pulled out of both the 50 cc and 125 cc categories, but continued to employ Ralph Bryans and Mike Hailwood in other classes. Hailwood took the 350 cc world title with ease, adding the 250 cc crown after victory by the slimmest of margins over Phil Read. Agostini once again triumphed over Hailwood and Honda in the 500 class.

By now Honda had achieved their basic objective. Gaining international fame on the race circuits of the world had created a vast sales potential which was to enable the organisation to develop into the biggest motor cycle business ever known. The massive investment in racing which they had ungrudgingly made had paid off and there was no further need, from a commercial point of view, for them to pursue with all the urge and fanaticism for which they had become known, those expensive world championships.

The 500 cc world title was always to escape them. Even when they bought Mike Hailwood they couldn't buy success. Although their failure in this category remained privately a bitter disappointment, it was perhaps little enough price to have to pay when set against their overwhelming triumphs in other directions.

# 15
# The Feud that made the Headlines

The idea of riding to team orders has always been a thorny problem. It challenges the widely accepted idea that in racing you always go all out to win. Surely, that is what racing is about. So when in 1968 Phil Read refused to let Bill Ivy win the 250 cc World Title – and went on to secure the honours for himself – he created a sensation.

The feud which developed between Read and Ivy as a result was bitter and uncompromising. Phil's action also brought to the surface the whole obscure business of riding, not for yourself, but for the good of the factory that sponsors you.

Many riders, more in the know about off-track politics than the average spectator, didn't quite see what all the public fuss was about. Riding to orders, though officially condemned by the governing bodies of the sport, was known to go on and had been quietly part of team racing from much earlier days.

Stanley Woods said that, so far as he knew, team riding was introduced into motor cycle racing in 1931 by Nortons. 'The man who pays the piper calls the tune,' he told *Motor Cycle*. 'So manufacturers who spend many thousands of pounds on racing must be able to demand a certain amount of team discipline.'

Woods conceded that the public wouldn't be aware what was going on, but even when the great Stanley Woods was at his peak the natural instinct for a man always to give of his best and race all out to win was shown to be a driving urge not easily controlled. As Woods said when invited by *Motor Cycle* to comment on the Read-Ivy controversy: 'I was a professional rider and the financial aspect of riding to orders wasn't doing

me any good, though I loved every minute of racing. It all
came to a head at the Ulster in 1933 when Nortons made it
clear that I wasn't to win the 500 cc class. As it turned out I did
win and I didn't have to disobey orders to do it because Tim
(Hunt) broke down. But I left Nortons after that and never rode
to orders again.'

Similar views on the rights of a factory to instruct its riders
were voiced by both Geoff Duke and Mike Hailwood. Geoff
said that from a manufacturers point of view, riding to orders
was essential. Mike said that when a team had two riders of
similar ability they *must* ride to orders to prevent them falling
off or blowing up their machines unnecessarily.

What seemed odd in the Yamaha Read/Ivy sensation was
that the Japanese factory was vitually assured of both the 125
cc and 250 cc world titles, in addition to the manufacturers
trophy, so why not let the best man win.

This, in fact, was Phil Read's point and he made it conclusively by stating publicly that he would race to win ... or
quit.

Brilliant displays by both Phil Read and Bill Ivy towards the
end of 1967 made them almost automatic choices for the
Yamaha team for 1968. The previous season had seen Bill
secure the 125 cc title for Yamaha, but it was said to have been
obvious to observers who were sufficiently experienced to de-
tect such things, that he had deliberately eased back in one or
two of the 250 cc races in order to let Phil cross the line first.

Perhaps this was the start of the trouble which was to come.
Bill unquestionably was rapidly making an impact on the racing
scene and was accepted by Yamaha as a brilliant racer with
almost limitless potential. On peak form, he conveyed an impression of near invincibility. He had obviously impressed
Yamaha enormously and on the eye of the 1968 season was
possibly hotter property than Phil, who could not have been too
happy at the prospect, as advanced by Mick Woollett in *Motor
Cycle*, that Bill and not Phil was to be Yamaha's first string for
the new season.

It is easy to look back and make sensible assessments. At
the time you can only see the past and not the future. At the
approach to the 1968 season the possibility of Ivy becoming
first string did not cause much excitement. He had raced magni-

ficently to take the world title in 1967 while Phil, perhaps a little out of form and certainly going through one of those periods of ill-luck which come periodically to every racer, had struggled to tame the Yamaha four, only to see the prospect of a third world title denied him as Hailwood on the Honda took the honours.

The new season began with some exhilarating racing between the two Yamaha aces, competition being razor sharp. At Nürburgring in West Germany Bill was in sensational form, establishing a new race record in the 250 cc event and setting up new record laps in both the 125 and 250 cc races. Engine problems in Spain reduced the excitement, but in the TT Bill and Phil produced sparkling form, Bill pulling out the fastest lap at 100.32 mph in the 125 cc event and finishing second, while Phil won the race to record his third 125 cc TT victory in four years. In the 250 cc race, Phil's Yamaha punctured and he was forced to retire. Bill produced an incredible performance, winning the event and establishing a new lap record at 105.51 mph.

It was during the TTs that comment was first made about the Yamaha pair riding to a pattern. There was talk in the motor cycle press about their 'team plan', and one paper asked whether or not they were riding to team orders. Of course, no one said openly that they were, but a lot of people connected with racing had their own ideas, in spite of the keen competition and glorious sparring produced by Ivy and Read. There was more great racing in Holland, with Bill taking the 250 cc and Phil riding second. Phil won the 125 cc.

The situation was hotting up now and within weeks was to explode into the racing controversy of the decade, with Phil at the centre, and the obvious row with Bill over who should win was out in the open for all to see.

In the Czech Grand Prix, the seventh round of the world championship, Phil seemingly ignored the team plan and took first place in the 250 cc event. With John Cooper's Padgett-Yamaha stranded on the line, Read catapulted into the lead at the start and was never seriously challenged. Ivy, with Rosner's MZ revving at his shoulder for most of the race, did not shake clear until near the end. Although he closed the space between himself and Phil, he was unable to make a serious challenge.

Bill was angry and said so, claiming that the plan was that wherever possible he would take the 250 cc events while Phil made sure of the 125 cc races. Completing a bad day for Bill, and adding further insult to his pride, was his fall in the 125 cc event, which, he claimed, had been the result of avoiding action he had taken when he thought he saw Phil's rear wheel beginning to slide. Said Bill: 'I saw Read's rear wheel start to slide and I thought he was coming off. I took avoiding action. I thought that we would both come off, but when I looked round for Phil he wasn't there.'

Phil secured a comfortable victory in this race and then snatched a win in the 250 cc event which Bill felt was rightly his.

At this stage in the season the opportunity for Phil Read to secure an outstanding double world crown was obvious. In the 125 cc class he was well clear of all opposition, 28 points ahead and just one victory away from the title. In the 250 cc category only two points separated the team riders. In the manufacturers section Yamaha had 40 points, with MZ their nearest rival, down at 22 points.

At the same time, Bill Ivy faced the grim prospect of missing both titles.

Within a few days the situation had erupted with Read stating: 'I ride to win or quit.' This followed receipt of a cable from Japan, a cable which may have resulted from an official complaint to the factory which Bill had made following the Czechoslovakian Grand Prix.

Phil advanced a number of arguments in his favour. By now the manufacturers title had been clinched, he said, and added that once that had been decided he thought it was everyone for himself. 'I'd rather not ride if I have to finish second,' he said.

It was a gigantic wrangle. Read said he had cabled Japan with his version of the Czech incident, and added: 'Having stuck my neck out to help develop the Yamaha fours I want an equal chance now that they're good. If Bill reckons he can beat me, let him try.'

Ivy retorted: 'I've let Phil win the 125 cc title. Why shouldn't he let me win the 250? I fell off in Czechoslovakia because I slowed down to follow him. I only wish this business had hap-

pened earlier in the year. Then we'd have found out who was
the better rider.'

The situation was tense and fiery. There was a lot at stake.
Many comments were undoubtedly made in the heat of the
moment.

That there was open conflict between the two riders, however, was now beyond doubt. Any influence which the Yamaha
factory had on their riders earlier in the season was gone as
Read and Ivy prepared to battle it out for the remainder of the
year.

The immediate issue was the entries for the Ulster Grand
Prix in August. Apparently the original plan had been for both
Phil and Bill to contest only the 250 cc event, and Phil had sent
off entries on this basis. According to race secretary Bill
McMaster, reported in the motor cycle press, there was a later
phone call from Bill in which he said that Read had no
authority to fix his starts and said he wanted to compete in the
125 cc race as well. When Phil got to know what had happened,
he too filed his entry for the 125 cc event.

Sensational enough, but more was to follow. First the riders
clashed in Finland and the whole sport caught its breath as
Read and Ivy lined up for the 125 event. Read rocketed ahead
at the start, gaining a 200 yard lead, but Ivy was very much in
the race. After seven laps he was up in Phil's slipstream and the
tension was mounting. At the time he wanted it most, luck
deserted little Bill. He was forced to stop for adjustments to his
front brake and Phil did not need prodding to take his chance.
He romped on to win and secure the 125 cc crown.

Rain just before the 250 cc race made the track slippery and
in spite of their almost obsessional will to win, both Read and
Ivy, up at the front from the start, were forced to travel
cautiously. Ivy had been fractionally ahead for some time when,
on the eighth lap, Read made his move and opened up a 20
yards lead. It happened on a downhill right-hander, when Read
outbraked Ivy. Bill over-reached himself in a desperate attempt
to make up lost ground and spun off. The luckless Ivy aggra-
vated a leg he had injured in Czechoslovakia.

It was Read's day. He had won both races, overhauled the
existing 125 cc lap record by four seconds, and clinched the
125 cc world championship. His win in the 250 cc event also

meant that he was now ahead of Ivy in the race for that crown. Bill, on the other hand, had seemingly been struggling against ill-luck since before the race began. In his attempt to combat the all-out challenge from Phil, he had reportedly taken out a new Norton front fork in an effort to improve the 250 Yamaha's handling, and had hoped also to have a new exhaust system to give more bottom-end power. But the fork wouldn't fit and the exhaust system didn't arrive.

Bill's fans were distraught; Phil's elated. By now the feud which was openly being waged had brought out the crowds in legions, ranged up against each other ready to do battle on behalf of their heroes. But in the midst of everything, fresh news dominated. Sensationally, an ultimatum was issued to Yamaha from the Ulster Grand Prix authorities. The substance of the ultimatum was that unless the Japanese factory revoked any alleged orders to Phil Read to comply with their demands and ease back from his all-out onslaught on the 250 cc title, their entries for the Ulster would be cancelled.

Rightly sensitive to the public image of motor cycle racing, the FIM had been concerned about the question of team instructions, and had been working to make sure that genuine races were being run. It was said, for instance, that before the race in Finland, the FIM's sporting committee's president had spoken to Phil Read, reminding him that rules required riders to make a genuine effort. Any action directing a rider not to win races was, according to the FIM, illegal so far as the FIM regulations were concerned.

So Phil now was in a difficult position. Having brought the matter into the open, he knew Yamaha's views, and at the same time he was left in no doubt that if he did not ride to win he would face possible disciplinary action from the FIM. However this gave Phil a clear mandate to go ahead and do just that – ride to win.

It was later suggested that the FIM attitude could be considered hypocritical, as they were close enough to racing to know that factory instructions were commonplace, yet were willing to let the practice continue until someone brought it all out into the open.

It is difficult to know exactly the nature of the response the FIM attitude provoked from Japan, but over in Ireland the fans were wild with expectation as it became clear that both Read and Ivy would be contesting the 125 cc and 250 cc events. Bill desperately needed a 250 cc victory to stay in the running for the title and would probably need to win at the last Grand Prix of the season at Monza in order to clinch it. Never before had the Ulster been anticipated with greater excitement, and these two outstanding hell raisers produced the kind of riding that had taken them to world class ... fearless, fast and close.

The way Bill fought to win the 125 cc race made it difficult to think that, in terms of the world championship, that particular battle had been won and lost in Finland. But there was a psychological fight to be fought with thousands of fans picking up every move, and both Bill and Phil knew it. The race with real meaning was the 250, but this 125 event would do a lot to set the pattern for the afternoon.

The lap record, down to Bill at the start, was to be slashed time and again by both riders as they hurtled round the 7.4 miles Dundrod circuit. The vast crowd thrilled to sensational riding and in spite of a speed of 102.44 mph by Phil for a new lap record, Bill rode through in first position.

The victory gave Bill back some of his lost confidence. Phil too had ridden magnificently. The tension was almost unbearable as the two giants wheeled out their machines for the all-important 250.

This was the big one and as the flag dropped the crowd gasped as Phil was seen to be in the lead, but Bill was close to his elbow. The roads were wet and Phil pulled out all his skill and courage in an attempt to clear space between his Yamaha and the screaming two-stroke of Bill close behind. But Ivy hung on grimly. Round and round they screamed and then, as the crowd held its breath, Bill shot into the lead with Phil pounding after him. This time it was Bill's day and while he rode on to score a magnificent victory with a new record lap at 103.64 mph, Phil's challenge disappeared as a stone kicked up, cracked his radiator, and his engine seized.

Ivy now had 46 points, Read 44 and the last race of the season at Monza was the biggest one of all. By this time any ideas that either rider was prepared to race to orders were totally out of the question. Phil had thrown down the gauntlet and Bill had accepted the challenge. It was a tough, bitter fight and they didn't care who knew it. The only concern for them both was that 250 cc World Championship.

Monza was wet and miserable and once again it was Bill Ivy who thrashed ahead in the 125 event to win, while Phil, battling to make progress through the field, came off, though luckily was uninjured. He remounted and as if to demonstrate that his fall had done nothing to unnerve him for the 250 race to follow, managed to finish second at an average speed of 90.32 mph against Bill's 105.96. Bill was now riding with supreme confidence and fantastic skill and courage, and he set up the fastest lap in the 125 at 108.75 mph.

But now came the race which was to decide everything. It was as if every ounce of controversy and hostility which had surrounded the Read/Ivy feud over the last few months was telescoped into the all-out action of that Italian 250 Grand Prix. This would decide all issues. If Phil could succeed he would be a double World Champion, a magnificent achievement. If Bill failed he would finish with nothing. Those were the issues.

Events were to show how the entire situation remained charged with sensation until well after the race had ended. From the beginning the battle was on with Phil moving into the lead and Bill immediately behind, as in the 125 race. For three laps there was little to choose, but then as in any combat where the rivalry is so intense and the sides so evenly balanced, it became clear who the winner would be. In an effort to wrest the lead, Bill had to fight hard to keep control of his bike and he was fortunate not to take a tumble. In such razor sharp competition such a falter can be decisive, as it proved to be. Phil had palpitations as he encountered mechanical trouble towards the end of the race, but he needn't have worried. This wasn't Bill's day. Hampered by a machine which had gone bad on him, he even had trouble in taking second place.

So Phil Read had won ... but wait: Read and Ivy now had the same number of points. Moreover they had the same number of 'places' to their credit and the same number of 'placed' races. The Championship had to be decided on the respective times in each of the four races in which both had finished. This showed Phil better by a little over 2 minutes ... and he was declared World Champion!

But was he?...for Bill had taken the most extraordinary action immediately after the 250 event. Even while the riders were lining up for the 500 cc scrap, Bill scribbled a note of protest against Phil alleging that the front number plate of Read's Yamaha did not conform to FIM regulations and that his chain was not of the make he was contracted to use.

If the objections were upheld Phil would have to forfeit the world title he now claimed was his. Bill's action looked like a last-ditch attempt to deprive Phil of the title, but important races before had been won and lost on technicalities. In this case, however, the clerk of the course overruled Ivy's objection and Read *was* World Champion.

Phil, aghast at Ivy's behaviour, said he couldn't imagine anyone making such a transparent protest. Bill was unrepentant. He claimed he had nothing to lose and that Phil had stated before the race that if he (Bill) won, he would object that Ivy was under the FIM weight limit of 9 st. 6 lb.

It was an astonishing climax to one of the biggest sensations in motor cycle sport. Monza, which decided the honours for 1968, was to be the last time Phil Read and Bill Ivy raced together for Yamaha. As Phil had suspected earlier in the season, Yamaha were to retire from full-time factory sponsorship.

When the Read/Ivy rivalry was first brought to the public's attention during the early part of that significant 1968 season, it was by no means certain that we had not all been set-up by the Yamaha pair as part of a clever and cunning publicity stunt to keep the racing alive. They had been firm friends. They had shared many glorious triumphs. They were part of the same firm. With plenty of rounds still to be run, it was certain that, some unanticipated disaster apart, Yamaha would take the 125 and the 250 cc classes and also the manufacturer's prize. A deliberately engineered rift between two such big names was certain to pull attention back to a couple of race classes which were in danger of losing much of their edge, much too early on in the season, because the outcome was predictable.

By the end of the year, any such views had disappeared. At Monza no one could fail to see the gulf which had developed between the two, and if Yamaha wanted publicity they certainly got more than they can possibly have dared to hope for in 1968.

In the end Bill Ivy's desperate fight to keep faith with the original plan won him nothing. He had failed to secure the title, and wasn't able to find consolation in a public condemnation of Phil's action, for in December, when Yamaha summoned Read to Japan, there was no suggestion that it was in any way a disciplinary move, and it was widely believed that on his winning of the double world crown he had received a telegram of congratulations from Japan. This supreme Yamaha triumph transcended all other issues.

The few hectic months of bristling feud wrote themselves permanently into the history of motor cycle racing.

At the time a great deal was said and written about who was wrong and what should have been done. Bill was criticised for his protests which, suggested one columnist, had lost him the sympathy of many enthusiasts. Another sprang to his defence condemning, when Bill appeared at Oulton Park in September, the fans who booed him. He said they ought to be ashamed of themselves, that their action was disgusting and inexcusable.

If it can be said that a feud of this kind produces any sort of materialistic winner, then Phil Read must certainly be given that status. He finished the season with two world championships and had not appeared to prejudice his relations with Yamaha, though perhaps these were not so important as the Japanese factory had already relinquished its interest in all-out factory support to a team of riders. In fact in his book *Prince of Speed*, Phil significantly makes the point that towards the end of 1968 he had good reason to believe that Yamaha would follow the other big Japanese factories and withdraw from the grand prix scene. He goes on: 'It became more evident to me that this would be my last chance of regaining the world 250 crown that Mike Hailwood won from me.' Read said he made Bill Ivy fully aware of his decision so that he had a fair chance of beating Read in the remaining rounds of the championship.

Phil also revealed that as far as Yamaha was concerned the world championships had already ended at Brno. 'I knew that this meeting (Czechoslovakia) was to be the last which would be given official financial backing by the Yamaha concern during 1968. This meant that any further participation we made in the world championship series would have to be met and paid for by ourselves.'

Phil made his decision, decided to make a break for it and pulled off the double. For Bill it was an unworthy turning point in a short, but brilliant career. He lost the 250 cc title which he firmly believed he should have had, he was provoked because of it into making protests, and although he won later races in Britain, the season ended with his biting condemnation of the race game . . . and his retirement.

Riding to team instructions, the issue which had aroused such anger and stimulated such intense rivalry, had largely been lost in the claims and counter claims of the personalities of the piece, but once the fire of the moment had gone, fans were left to wonder to what extent Grand Prix racing generally had taken them for a ride.

Bertie Mann, a past president of the Motor Cycle Union of Ireland, commented at the time: 'Surely things have come to a sorry state in world championship racing when we have two champions openly arguing as to who wins what. It has been an open secret for years that this has been practised in manufacturers' teams and, for obvious reasons, it is probably unavoidable. But at least the organisers and public have been spared confirmation of this.'

Mann went on to suggest that now such tactics were generally known they must stop if the world championships were to count for anything.

These and similar comments made by a number of riders and others closely associated with racing were received with shock and disillusionment by many fans who get excited at the sight of a race bike ridden fast, pay their money to attend meetings and, surprising as it may seem, feel they are witnessing an event in which it is always the aim of every rider – even a works rider – to reach the finish first.

To this extent the Read/Ivy feud was a sobering lesson, as well as a major sensation.

F

# 16

# The Great Races

There was so much racing of quality, style, daring and spectacle in the 'sixties that it is almost impossible to know where to begin. Much of the best action centred around the world championship duels of Read and Redman, Hailwood and Agostini, but many other riders rode magnificent races in less headline-making circumstances and in less auspicious events.

At the beginning of the decade we thrilled to the superlative skills of such stars as John Surtees and Bob McIntyre, Derek Minter and Gary Hocking, Ubbiali of Italy, Fath and Duebel of West Germany. But if we move on to 1966 perhaps the start would be made with the historic TT victory by Agostini when he became the first Continental rider to win the Junior TT. It was a magnificent performance, for Ago, without the incentive of Hailwood breathing down his neck (Mike retired with engine trouble early in the race), produced new lap and race records. It was at these 1966 TTs that Hailwood reached his ninth TT victory, a superlative performance in the 500 cc race in which he rushed ahead to a 100 yards lead at the start over his starting partner, Joe Dunphy on a Norton. It was difficult to know who was winning on corrected times, but as the race progressed it became clear that Hailwood and Agostini were the two riders in contention for first place. Both were going well, but as rain lashed part of the course on the last few laps and Hailwood all but lost it when battling to control a sliding MV at Ramsey, Ago was still pushing hard; but Mike rode through to win.

Remember the phenomenal curtain-raiser to the 1966 season at Brands Hatch? In almost every event there were breathtaking moments, with honours going like this: Scivyer (Honda) 125 cc; Robb (Bultaco) 250 cc; Ivy (AJS-Metisse) 350 cc: Minter (Matchless) 500 cc; Butcher (650 Domiracer) 1,000 cc; Seeley and Rawlings (BMW) 1,300 cc sidecar; Vincent and Harrison (BSA) sidecar handicap. The most exciting event in a breakneck afternoon was perhaps the 1,000 cc class. Into the lead and going like a demon was John Cooper, but then it was wee Bill Ivy in the lead. Minter, contrary to form, was also mixing it among the leaders early on in the race and Griff Jenkins and Rex Butcher were also well placed. At half distance Rex stormed into the lead, and a momunental scrap now developed between Butcher and Ivy. Further down the field Minter and Cooper were locked in a similar battle. The final lap was packed with excitement as riders nosed ahead only to be retaken within a few yards. Butcher sneaked past Ivy to win, with Cooper, Minter and Jenkins, who had put up the fastest lap time, coming home in that order.

It was in 1966 that Bill Ivy became King of Brands for the first time in the new King of Brands event. In '65 Derek was supreme and, in a dazzling display of riding before a vast crowd, won three of the big races – an outstanding performance. But a year later it was Bill's day. Poor Derek, on his Seeley Matchless, had to retire, as did Griff Jenkins and Rex Butcher, but Bill rode ahead of a magnificent Dave Degens when Dave, in sensational form, unfortunately missed gears and allowed the Maidstone rider to go through.

The great races were not exclusive to Britain. At Imola, in Italy, Agostini came back in sensational form after a crash at Cervia just seven days before to pulverise his great rivals Tarquinio Provini (Benelli) and Mike Hailwood (Honda) in the 350 cc event, and to gain another great victory in the 500 cc race, winning against the surprise outing on a factory Gilera four of Derek Minter.

Bill Ivy's first classic win came in Spain in May, 1966. Riding a water-cooled twin-cylinder Yamaha Bill dominated a 125 cc race in which Taveri and Bryans were second and third, and Read on the other Yamaha fourth.

Four months later it was Agostini again in sensational form at Monza, riding to success in a 500 cc event which was to clinch for him the World Championship, the first Italian to win the 500 cc title since Liberati in 1957. Ago also romped home first in the 350 cc outing, breaking lap and race records.

That year Agostini won the Race of the Year at Mallory

Park, cruel luck dissipating a Hailwood challenge. Reputedly receiving the highest start money ever paid to any rider in Britain, Ago was lucky to come away with the £1,000-plus prize money. A mix-up on the starting grid put Agostini towards the back and Hailwood, on the Honda six, was on the back row! But so explosive was Mike's start that he had rocketed to the front before the first bend! Ago, unfamiliar with the tactics necessary to break clear of such bunching of riders, had difficulty weaving his way through the field and did not really see daylight for five laps, by which time Mike was some 14 seconds in the lead. Ago, now moving well, took a sprinting Ron Chandler and Dave Degens in one lap, but had more difficulty in overhauling Peter Williams and Bill Ivy to move into second place.

With only Hailwood up ahead, Ago on the MV began to make progress, reducing the space between them. Mike, sensing danger, accepted the challenge and opened up the lead again. With only seven laps remaining, Mike's rear tyre punctured and he had to retire.

Hailwood and Agostini had by now built up a reputation for keen rivalry. It was obvious that they should. Both had powerful machines in the 350 and 500 cc classes; both were glamorous, bachelor-gay works riders; both globe-trotted continuously and were present, side by side, at most of the big races of the day. Each had a healthy respect for the other's talents and skills. Because of machine failures and the inability of the Honda camp to make the big Honda more reliable, Ago almost always had the edge over Mike, but this did not detract from the excitement the two generated among crowds whenever they were down on the card to ride against each other. Mike had been bitterly disappointed with the Honda's performance in 1966 and started 1967 determined to win back the 500 cc world title. In West Germany he was in the lead when a broken crankshaft put him out of the race. In a dramatic TT in which Mike suffered from a loose twist-grip and finally Ago's rear chain broke, Hailwood came out the winner. The ding-dong battle was fought over and over again as the Grand Prix season wore on and towards the end it seemed that Mike would have his way.

It was at Monza a year earlier that Mike's title hopes had run aground. Monza it seemed would again scuttle his hopes.

Hailwood roared away to build up a tremendous lead, but with only three laps separating him from the championship, the Honda stuck in sixth gear and Mike was out of the race.

The following year brought many epic victories and a number of racing milestones. Bill Ivy gained a dramatic Grand Prix double, Minter said he wanted to win the King of Brands crown again, didn't, and, later in the year, retired; and Hurricane Hailwood, as he was now being dubbed, rushed to his 10th TT victory.

It was left to Mike to create one of the early-season sensations on the track when riding magnificently at Oulton Park. Having won the 350 cc race, he set off in search of a 250 cc victory, but the Honda six got the better of him and he hit the ground. He picked himself up, got the machine going again and in winning the race also set up the fastest lap of the day. It was an incredible performance.

Three days earlier, Derek Minter's hopes as he prepared for the King of Brands title were not to be realised. Ron Chandler took the title. Derek, in the earlier 350 cc race, came in third, but a damaged wrist from which he was recovering did not stand the strain well and he had to withdraw from the 'King' event.

John Cooper showed just how much of a master of Mallory he was when he won the title race of the day. Determined Cooper gunned his Norton into an early lead, even ahead of the 350 Honda of Hailwood. The day produced rain, sleet and even snow, but the riders battled on. Up with Cooper challenging for the lead were Chandler, Pat Mahoney and Alan Barnett. John Blanchard forced his Seeley Matchless up among them, but the effort was just too much. He lost it at the hairpin, fell off and broke his collarbone.

Hailwood, meantime, with an ailing machine, was dropping well back and had the ignominious experience of being lapped by the leaders! When that had last happened to Mike nobody could remember. But as the rain eased and the track dried, Mike fought hard and rode brilliantly. The finish was unexpected and sensational. As the chequered flag was held out for Cooper just behind Mike but a lap ahead, Mike went through and rode straight back into the paddock. He had forgotten he

was one lap behind, so officially he was classed as having retired.

Bill Ivy's first double Grand Prix victory came at Clermont-
Ferrand. The early part of the 250 cc race was a prodigious
battle. Ivy and Phil Read, on Yamahas, led Mike Hailwood's
Honda six for the first few laps, but Mike managed to overhaul
them and, with a record lap of 83.42 mph, pulled well ahead.
Fortunes then changed, as all three machines were beset with
mechanical touble. First it was Mike. He lost gears as he was
accelerating out of a corner and had to limp tamely round to the
start where the Honda mechanics worked like demons to sort
out the problem. In the meantime, Phil Read was in trouble.
His clutch wasn't working properly. Ivy, consequently, was
well up now, just behind Phil. Mike's Honda was put right and
he restarted just as Phil was coming round.

Now Mike and Phil were side by side and Ivy was close at
hand. First Hailwood was in front, then Read, but as both
struggled with gear changes on a corner, Bill Ivy dashed ahead
to reach the line first. Afterwards, Bill admitted that *his* bike
had been misfiring and at one point he had almost pulled into
the pits and retired. It's not often you get the opportunity of
winning when saddled with such a lame bike.

Bill had been experiencing misfiring problems in the earlier
125 cc event. But the trouble seemed to clear itself and Bill,
though hard pressed by Katayama on a Suzuki twin, began to
pull away. With a remarkable display of riding Ivy heeled the
Yamaha well over as he chased the race leaders and began to
move up to the front. He becme the front runner at the half
way stage and on that same lap created a new lap record.

Ivy, at about this time, was making the motor cycle world
sit up and take notice. At the Isle of Man, riding his 250 cc
Yamaha, he reached a phenomenal 153.8 mph going through
*Motor Cycling's* speed trap, faster than the speeds reached
only the year before by the giant 500 cc MV and Honda, but
it was Hailwood who won the race and so equalled the record
of ten TT victories set up in 1939 by the great Stanley Woods.

It was an outstanding victory. Ivy and Read pushed him very
hard, but Mike, despite handling problems on the Honda, led
the race from beginning to end and, in addition to equalling
Woods' record, also established new lap and race records.

What a week it was to be for Hailwood. He followed his 250 cc win with victories in the 350 and 500 cc events, establishing an all-time record of 12 TT victories and his second TT hat-trick. Mike, in victory, admitted that had not Agostini's chain snapped after five laps, he doubted that he could have won. Mike's loose throttle was forcing him to ride virtually one handed.

The 1967 TTs commemorated the Diamond Jubilee of racing on the Isle of Man and the Senior event, contested so competitively by Hailwood and Agostini, was a fitting testimony to such a milestone. As Robin Miller so excitingly described in *Motor Cycle News*: 'The two greatest riders in the world, Mike Hailwood and Giacomo Agostini, hurling their 160 mph machines round the greatest course in the world . . . yes, this was the greatest race in the world. Has there ever been such savage spectacle, such sensational, soul-shattering speed as in this 1967 Senior TT?'

A couple of months later, Mike had a narrow escape from serious injury when riding in the Finnish Grand Prix at Imatra. A downpour as the 500 cc race began, which many believe should have forced a suspension of the event, made the track particularly treacherous and Mike came to grief as he urged the big Honda through a corner at about 70 mph. Mike couldn't keep it on the track and it careered into one of the trackside trees. The machine was a heap of rubble, but Mike emerged little the worse for a nasty experience. He even went on to race – and to win – the 250 cc event held shortly afterwards.

Meantime, at home circuits, the fabulous Derek Minter was back to something like his old form. And where else but Brands Hatch should he choose to remind his fans that there was plenty of fire in the old lad yet? In a sensational 500 cc race he climbed from eighth position on the first lap to overhaul riders of the calibre of John Cooper, Ron Chandler and Dave Croxford and streak ahead to win. It was all the more remarkable because Derek had sustained a crushed foot at the start when another rider's wheel had come too close, and had to get someone to push him off. Derek had already declared his intention of retiring at the end of the season, but went on to remind his fans of all his old glories of a few years ago.

Early in October that year he went to Snetterton and in a

beautiful display of riding broke the lap record in the 500 cc heat, and rode out a classy winner in the 500 cc final.

Later that same month Derek crowned a superlative career with two memorable wins at Brands Hatch in his last afternoon of competitive racing. He rode to glory in the 350 cc events and almost snatched a third victory in the 500 cc final.

As in every decade, the 'sixties produced individual heroes, all of whom rode great races in the opinions of their supporters. So who were the great racers of the 'sixties? Among the Hailwoods and the Agostinis, the Reads, Ivys, Minters and Redmans, let us not forget the significant deeds in the early 'sixties by such talented riders as Carlo Ubbiali, Helmut Fath, Gary Hocking and, of course, the immortal John Surtees. Later there came Degner, Anderson and Taveri, Scheidegger, Enders and Deubel. There was Colin Seeley, Paul Smart, Paddy Driver, Alan Shepherd, John Cooper, Dan Shorey, Peter Inchley, Griff Jenkins, Tommy Robb, Derek Chatterton, Chris Vincent, Chris Conn, Ray Pickrell, John Hartle, John Blanchard, Mike Duff and many, many others including speed and sprint men like Bob Leppan, Bill Johnson, Alf Hagon and George Brown.

Surely one of the most convincing and hoped-for victories of all time was that of John Hartle at Mallory Park in March 1968. John, back at the track where he had been seriously injured, fought an unnerving and emotional situation to win a fine 350 cc event. It was a nervous moment for us all as John lined up for the start. Our anxieties were unfounded. Hartle stormed away with a great deal of confidence and won by three seconds. The sensations of the afternoon were provided by the sidecar men. There were lucky escapes from two fearsome crashes for Peter Brown and David Bean, Mick Boddice and Dave Loach. Dave sustained a broken ankle.

Hartle rode brilliantly again, this time at Brands Hatch in March 1968, to win the 100-mile 500 cc Redex Grand National.

There was plenty of great racing when the West German Grand Prix returned to the Nürburgring after a three year absence. Five of the six short-lap records were excelled and the sixth was equalled. Man of the meeting was Agostini who, in a scorching ride on the 350 cc MV, took six seconds off Mike Hailwood's 500 cc lap record set only three years earlier. Bill Ivy also rode brilliantly, setting up new lap records in the 125 cc and 250 cc events. Bill won the latter, Phil Read going ahead to win in the 125 cc.

At the TTs in 1968 it was Bill Ivy who created the first sensations. In the 250 cc class Ivy on the works four-cylinder Yamaha smashed Mike Hailwood's 250 cc Mountain Circuit lap record by more than 12 seconds, reaching over 105 mph. The race was a thriller with Bill riding out as winner on a Yamaha limping with a fractured expansion chamber after Phil Read had retired with a puncture. During practice, Ivy became the first man to lap the course at over 100 mph on a 125 cc machine.

At Brands Hatch Mike Hailwood bettered Derek Minter's five year old absolute record by just six tenths of a second and a sensational hat-trick of wins at Mallory Park by John Cooper was all the more remarkable as, following a crash in the Ulster, he hadn't intended riding again that season, but was persuaded to have this one outing at his 'home' circuit. In shattering form he won the 250, 350 and 500 cc events.

As the last season of the 'sixties was beginning to run out, let us look again at Agostini scoring a double victory in Spain after falling twice, and creating the first 130 mph lap ever in a Grand Prix.

At the Jarma circuit, Agostini was pushing ahead in the 500 cc race intent on catching early leaders Bergamonti and Kel Carruthers. On a corner Carruthers lost control and came off. Ago, following close behind, hurtled into Kel's Aermacchi and he too came off. With Carruthers' aid, Ago got the powerful MV upright again and after dusting himself down set off in pursuit of Bergamonti who had gained at least a mile through the incident. Agostini, though shaken, was determined and within seven more laps had caught and overtaken Bergamonti.

Two months later Agostini created race history when, at the Belgian Grand Prix, he hurried his MV four to a new Grand Prix record lap at more than 130 mph during his victory in the 500 cc class. It had taken twelve years for anyone to beat Bob McIntyre's famous Gilera ride of 129.55 mph at the West German Grand Prix of 1957, and in creating the new record Agostini lapped every other rider except one.

While it is true that the massive support of Honda and others in the 'sixties helped to create the right conditions for great racing, the contribution to this exciting period by sponsors, organisers, machine mechanics and tuners must not be overlooked; people like Geoff Monty, Tom Kirby, Syd Lawton, Steve Lancefield, Ray Petty and others. They were close to the action and often spoke out without fear on issues they felt to be important. They were very much part of the scene and mustn't be forgotten.

# 17
# Into the '70s...

As the 'sixties made way for a new era two important issues began to emerge in motor cycle racing. A much closer liaison between Britain, which for so long had restricted its overseas activities to Grand Prix racing mainly on the continent, and the United States became apparent; and the rumblings of criticism about the TT Races which had been heard quietly for years, began to break out thunderously into the open.

Daytona, the vast American race circuit with its sweeping speed stretches, came increasingly into our headlines. As early as April 1970 Paul Dunstall predicted that racing in Britain would become increasingly influenced by the sport in America. He said that the World Championships were dwindling in importance because the major factories, particularly the Japanese, were giving more of their concentration to the great sales potential of the American market.

This meant that racers whose names had become familiar to the British racing public were now beginning to make fairly regular trips to the United States. Take Daytona 1970 for example. Kel Carruthers was there on a 350 cc Yamaha. Mike Hailwood was astride a BSA. And the trend was the development of American aces coming to Britain to challenge the home-based experts on close-cornered short circuits like Brands Hatch and Mallory Park.

These considerably closer ties with America brought Mike Hailwood back into the news. There were stories of offers tempting him out of bike racing retirement – rides in America, a States series, an astonishing opportunity to earn something in the region of £40,000. But in February '71, Mike said that apart from a few chosen races he would not return to riding bikes. He had recently linked up with John Surtees in the car world and had high hopes of developing his career in that direction.

BSA-Triumph were now investing a lot of money in the American racing scene and Britain's Paul Smart, after a practice session on the sweeping Daytona circuit, was favourite to win the Daytona 200 on one of their machines. The expectation was not realised. After leading, Paul broke down and failed to finish, as did Mike Hailwood, who also led before retiring.

Although Smart was unsuccessful, racing in America was much to his liking. Although a non-finisher he made £1,500 out of the race, setting the fastest qualifying time and also being paid for each of the 31 laps in which he led the field.

This was the glossy type of American-style racing which was to attract British riders at the start of the 1970s. Plenty of money for the successful riders, smooth and slick off-track organisation, lots of sponsorship to be had, and comfortable luxury hotels in which to stay.

Britain's Anglo-American race series brought top-flight Americans to this country and while they had to acknowledge the superiority of British riders on our shorter circuits, their skill and daring showed through sufficiently to thrill the crowds and to give a hint or two that the British aces must not take the American challenge too lightly.

Such was the developing interest in the Daytona-style of racing that *Motor Cycle News* in 1971 inaugurated their £2,000 Superbike Championships covering six major international meetings.

By early 1972 John Player were sponsoring transatlantic road race series at Easter and fans thrilled to the sight of America's Cal Rayborn on a 750 Harley Davidson winning three of the six races. In America, British riders were making a name for themselves too. John Cooper, as mentioned in an earlier chapter, came through to win the Ontario meeting in 1971 and it was Paul Smart's turn in the same event in 1972, winning £12,000 at the rate of £70 a minute! Paul tied on points with New Zealander Geoff Perry, Paul on a Kawasaki and Perry on a Suzuki.

On a more traditional front, the legendary TTs were going through a bad patch. Criticised years earlier by such riders as Derek Minter and John Cooper for poor financial rewards and for not putting enough of the money made from the races back into them, the smouldering unrest broke to the surface during the early 'seventies. The gutsy earthiness of TT racing had always been one of its greatest attractions. There was something historic about the TT races, they were steeped in the tradition of the early days of the sport. But they were also tough and demanding and, according to a growing number of riders, downright dangerous. As early as 1966 the normally placid Agostini had criticised the TT circuit because of its dangers and said he did not think the medical services were all they might be.

Following a tragic TT fortnight in 1970 Kel Carruthers came out with a strong attack on the state of the 37¾-mile Mountain Circuit. After winning the 250 cc TT he said that he would not ride again in the TT races unless ordered to do so as a factory team member. And Rodney Gould said the circuit was in bad condition, very dangerous and hinted at a proposed boycott of riders for 1971 unless something more was done.

A year later, Agostini again protested against the TT course. He said the time had arrived when sweeping changes ought to be made as the present course had become far too dangerous. He wanted it shortened where safety standards common to other circuits could be maintained.

In 1972 Ago again attacked the TT and asked for it to be stripped of its world championship status. The comments were triggered by the fatal crash in the rain during the 125 cc event of his friend, fellow Italian Gilberto Parlotti. This was the 99th fatality in TT racing, and in 1970 no fewer than six riders had been killed in the Island's race packed fortnight.

Even stronger action followed. Phil Read said he had sent a letter to Prince Philip, the patron of the TT races, concerning the dangers of the course. Said Read: 'I have also inferred that it may not be complimentary for Prince Philip to be associated with a race which is such a killer.'

Not all riders, it should be said, held such critical views, and many officials and riders thought it virtually impossible to make the races safer. All the same, there was no doubt that the future of the TT races as we knew them was in danger and the next couple of years could be critical and decisive.

These fundamental issues apart, what had racing in the early 'seventies to offer? Of course, there was an exciting new crop of

Hell Raisers thirsting for the glamour and honour of winning races at high speed. Some of the stalwarts of the 'sixties remained, among them of course, Agostini, Phil Read and John Cooper, but new heroes included riders like Barry Sheene, Charles Mortimer, Tony Jeffries, Percy Tait and Rodney Gould. From Finland came a race sensation called Jarno Saarinen. He broke into motor cycling's headlines sensationally in May 1972 when he outpaced the virtually unbeatable MV of Agostini at the West German Grand Prix.

The 25-year-old Finn was dynamite and on a new water-cooled works Yamaha he had Ago well beaten, the first time for some five years that the handsome Italian had been forced to play second fiddle in a major race.

From that point on, one Saarinen sensation rapidly followed another at Silverstone against some outstanding opposition on powerful machinery, he collected three wins during the afternoon in the John Player international road races. The flying Finn shattered lap records and, only a week later, this time on a new four-cylinder Benelli, once again put it across Agostini. It seemed that after waiting for years for a really serious challenger, since the halcyon days of the Hailwood/Agostini duels, Ago might at last have met his match.

As the season drew to a close Saarinen was the name shouted by almost everyone. He shattered the opposition in Britain at the Rothman's Race of the Year at Mallory Park, knocking 1.4 seconds off the lap record. In this blistering race he brushed aside the tough challenge of Cal Rayborn from America; and even John Cooper, who knows Mallory better than anyone, could not top Jarno's incredible performance.

Closer ties with the United States; a challenge to the standing and even existence of the TT races as we knew them; new riders with dash and flair – this was the life-style of motor cycle racing in the early 1970s. But there were other incidents and developments. There was a walk-out by Phil Read and George Brown at Cadwell Park, a dispute concerning practice for Phil and over runs for George. The motor bike orientated movies continued with luscious Ann Margret, a great big bike fan, featured in a new picture called 'CC and Company'. Silverstone looked like recapturing some of its old time glory as a motor cycle race circuit, and Harley-Davidson, through

American Motorcycle Association racer Cal Rayborn, pushed the outright world speed record even higher.

In 1971 Norton revived an interest in big time racing, Ago was reduced to fourth place behind Paul Smart, Tony Rutter and Derek Chatterton at Cadwell Park, and there was criticism of the new type of close, fully-enclosed 'Ned Kelly' helmets which were now becoming more and more popular. Severe financial problems was responsible for a cut-back in the race programme of BSA and Barry Sheene, the twenty-year-old Londoner, got himself talked about with scintillating victories at the Hutchinson 100 at Brands Hatch, pushing ahead of such star talent as Phil Read, John Cooper and Rod Gould.

Tragedy at Oulton Park resulted in the deaths of three side-car riders, Rod Gould crashed in Holland, but escaped with only a torn arm muscle, and there were reports that nine-times world champion veteran Carlo Ubbiali was doing more than just thinking about making a come back.

Meantime, at the Grand Prix level, Phil Read was still riding triumphant and in 1971 took his fifth world championship.

In 1972 no one was really very surprised when the news was released that BSA-Triumph would not be fielding a racing team for the current year, because of a cut-back in the racing budget.

In America Don Emde won the 1972 Daytona 200 on a privately entered 350 cc Yamaha, while Yamaha star Phil Read won on an MV in the 350 cc East German Grand Prix.

The 'seventies sensation, Jarno Saarinen said he wanted more money or he would quit, and that if he was lucky enough to win a world title in 1972 he would retire. Fred Cooper reached 189 mph and in a flurry of speed mania, Honda, Bob Leppan and Norton Villiers were said to be intent on reaching for the world outright speed record.

Certainly, there was much going on in the high speed world of motor cycle racing in the 'seventies and if for some it lacked the vigour and vitality of the Grand Prix circus and the colourful characters of the swinging 'sixties, perhaps another exciting era was dawning with the news in 1972 that Taiwan Chinese machines were coming into Britain and, according to *Motor Cycle News,* a revolutionary Wankel engined, Chinese-built 500 cc roadster would arrive early in 1973.

# Appendix

## Road Racing World Champions

*Solo Classes 50* cc
1962    Ernst Degner, West Germany (Suzuki)
1963    Hugh Anderson, New Zealand (Suzuki)
1964    Hugh Anderson, New Zealand (Suzuki)
1965    Ralph Bryans, Ireland (Honda)
1966    Hans-Georg Anscheidt, W. Germany (Suzuki)
1967    Hans-Georg Anscheidt, W. Germany (Suzuki)
1968    Hans-Georg Anscheidt, W. Germany (Suzuki)
1969    Angel Nieto, Spain (Derbi)

*125 cc*
1960    Carlo Ubbiali, Italy (MV)
1961    Tom Phillis, Australia (Honda)
1962    Luigi Taveri, Switzerland (Honda)
1963    Hugh Anderson, New Zealand (Suzuki)
1964    Luigi Taveri, Switzerland (Honda)
1965    Hugh Anderson, New Zealand (Suzuki)
1966    Luigi Taveri, Switzerland (Honda)
1967    Bill Ivy, Britain (Yamaha)
1968    Phil Read, Britain (Yamaha)
1969    Dave Simmonds, Britain (Kawasaki)

*250 cc*
1960    Carlo Ubbiali, Italy (MV)
1961    Mike Hailwood, Britain (Honda)
1962    Jim Redman, Rhodesia (Honda)
1963    Jim Redman, Rhodesia (Honda)
1964    Phil Read, Britain (Yamaha)
1965    Phil Read, Britain (Yamaha)
1966    Mike Hailwood, Britain (Honda)
1967    Mike Hailwood, Britain (Honda)
1968    Phil Read, Britain (Yamaha)
1969    Kel Carruthers, Australia (Benelli)

*350 cc*
1960    John Surtees, Britain (MV)
1961    Gary Hocking, Rhodesia (MV)
1962    Jim Redman, Rhodesia (Honda)
1963    Jim Redman, Rhodesia (Honda)

1964 Jim Redman, Rhodesia (Honda)
1965 Jim Redman, Rhodesia (Honda)
1966 Mike Hailwood, Britain (Honda)
1967 Mike Hailwood, Britain (Honda)
1968 Giacomo Agostini, Italy (MV)
1969 Giacomo Agostini, Italy (MV)

*500 cc*
1960 John Surtees, Britain (MV)
1961 Gary Hocking, Rhodesia (MV)
1962 Mike Hailwood, Britain (MV)
1963 Mike Hailwood, Britain (MV)
1964 Mike Hailwood, Britain (MV)
1965 Mike Hailwood, Britain (MV)
1966 Giacomo Agostini, Italy (MV)
1967 Giacomo Agostini, Italy (MV)
1968 Giacomo Agostini, Italy (MV)
1969 Giacomo Agostini, Italy (MV)

*Sidecar Class 500 cc*
1960 Helmut Fath, W. Germany (BMW)
1961 Max Deubel, W. Germany (BMW)
1962 Max Deubel, W. Germany (BMW)
1963 Max Deubel, W. Germany (BMW)
1964 Max Deubel, W. Germany (BMW)
1965 Fritz Scheidegger, Switzerland (BMW)
1966 Fritz Scheidegger, Switzerland (BMW)
1967 Klaus Enders, W. Germany (BMW)
1968 Helmut Fath, W. Germany (URS)
1969 Klaus Enders, W. Germany (BMW)

# Official World Speed Records

| Date | Rider | Country and course where record set | | Machine | mph |
|---|---|---|---|---|---|
| 14.4.20 | E. Walker | U.S.A. | Daytona | 994 cc Indian | 103.5 |
| 9.9.23 | F. W. Dixon | France | Arpajon | 989 cc Harley-Davidson | 106.5 |
| 6.11.23 | C. F. Temple | England | Brooklands | 996 cc British-Anzani | 108.5 |
| 27.4.24 | H. Le Vack | France | Arpajon | 867 cc Brough Superior JAP | 113.5 |
| 6.7.24 | H. Le Vack | France | Arpajon | 867 cc Brough Superior JAP | 119 |
| 5.9.26 | C. F. Temple | France | Arpajon | 996 cc OEC Temple | 121.5 |
| 25.8.28 | O. M. Baldwin | France | Arpajon | 996 cc Zenith JAP | 124.5 |
| 25.8.29 | H. Le Vack | France | Arpajon | 995 cc Brough Superior JAP | 129 |
| 19.9.29 | E. Henne | Germany | Munich | 740 cc BMW | 134.5 |
| 31.8.30 | J. S. Wright | France | Arpajon | 994 cc OEC Temple JAP | 137.5 |
| 20.9.30 | E. Henne | Germany | Ingolstadt | 735 cc BMW | 137.5 |
| 6.11.30 | J. S. Wright | Ireland | Cork | 995 cc OEC Temple JAP | 150.5 |
| 3.11.32 | E. Henne | Hungary | Tat | 735 cc BMW | 152 |
| 28.10.34 | E. Henne | Hungary | Gyon | 735 cc BMW | 153 |
| 27.9.35 | E. Henne | Germany | Frankfurt a/M | 735 cc BMW | 159 |
| 12.10.36 | E. Henne | Germany | Frankfurt a/M | 495 cc BMW | 159 |
| 19.4.37 | E. Fernihough | Hungary | Gyon | 995 cc Brough Superior JAP | 169.5 |
| 21.10.37 | P. Taruffi | Italy | Brescia-Bergamo | 492 cc Gilera | 170.5 |
| 28.11.37 | E. Henne | Germany | Darmstadt | 495 cc BMW | 173.5 |
| 12.4.51 | W. Herz | Germany | Munich | 499 cc NSU | 180 |
| 2.7.55 | R. Wright | N. Zealand | Christchurch | 998 cc Vincent HRD | 185 |
| 2.8.56 | W. Herz | U.S.A. | Bonneville | 347 cc NSU | 189 |
| 4.8.56 | W. Herz | U.S.A. | Bonneville | 499 cc NSU | 210 |
| 5.9.62 | W. Johnson | U.S.A. | Bonneville | 667 cc Triumph | 224.5 |

# TT Races

| Year | Class | | Rider | Machine |
|------|-------|---|-------|---------|
| 1960 | Senior | 1 | J. Surtees | MV |
| | | 2 | J. Hartle | MV |
| | | 3 | S. M. B. Hailwood | Norton |
| | Junior | 1 | J. Hartle | MV |
| | | 2 | J. Surtees | MV |
| | | 3 | R. McIntyre | AJS |
| | Light-weight 250 cc | 1 | G. Hocking | MV |
| | | 2 | C. Ubbiali | MV |
| | | 3 | T. Provini | Morini |
| | Light-weight 125 cc | 1 | C. Ubbiali | MV |
| | | 2 | G. Hocking | MV |
| | | 3 | L. Taveri | MV |
| | Sidecar | 1 | H. Fath | BMW |
| | | 2 | P. V. Harris | BMW |
| | | 3 | C. Freeman | Norton |
| 1961 | Senior | 1 | S. M. B. Hailwood | Norton |
| | | 2 | R. McIntyre | Norton |
| | | 3 | T. E. Phillis | Norton |
| | Junior | 1 | P. W. Read | Norton |
| | | 2 | G. Hocking | MV |
| | | 3 | R. B. Rensen | Norton |
| | Light-weight 250 cc | 1 | S. M. B. Hailwood | Honda |
| | | 2 | T. E. Phillis | Honda |
| | | 3 | J. A. Redman | Honda |
| | Light-weight 125 cc | 1 | S. M. B. Hailwood | Honda |
| | | 2 | L. Taveri | Honda |
| | | 3 | T. E. Phillis | Honda |
| | Sidecar | 1 | M. Deubel | BMW |
| | | 2 | F. Scheidegger | BMW |
| | | 3 | P. V. Harris | BMW |
| 1962 | Senior | 1 | G. Hocking | MV |
| | | 2 | E. Boyce | Norton |
| | | 3 | F. J. Stevens | Norton |
| | Junior | 1 | S. M. B. Hailwood | MV |
| | | 2 | G. Hocking | MV |
| | | 3 | F. Stastny | Jawa |
| | Light-weight 250 cc | 1 | D. W. Minter | Honda |
| | | 2 | J. Redman | Honda |
| | | 3 | T. Phillis | Honda |
| | Light-weight 125 cc | 1 | L. Taveri | Honda |
| | | 2 | T. Robb | Honda |
| | | 3 | T. Phillis | Honda |

| Year | Class | Rider | Machine |
|------|-------|-------|---------|
| | 50 cc | 1 E. Degner | Suzuki |
| | | 2 L. Taveri | Honda |
| | | 3 T. Robb | Honda |
| | Sidecar | 1 C. Vincent | BSA |
| | | 2 O. Kolle | BMW |
| | | 3 C. J. Seeley | Matchless |
| 1963 | Senior | 1 S. M. B. Hailwood | MV |
| | | 2 J. Hartle | Gilera |
| | | 3 P. W. Read | Gilera |
| | Junior | 1 J. A. Redman | Honda |
| | | 2 J. Hartle | Gilera |
| | | 3 F. Stastny | Jawa |
| | Lightweight 250 cc | 1 J. A. Redman | Honda |
| | | 2 F. Ito | Yamaha |
| | | 3 W. A. Smith | Honda |
| | Lightweight 125 cc | 1 H. R. Anderson | Suzuki |
| | | 2 F. G. Perris | Suzuki |
| | | 3 E. Degner | Suzuki |
| | 50 cc | 1 M. Ito | Suzuki |
| | | 2 H. R. Anderson | Suzuki |
| | | 3 H. G. Anscheidt | Kreidler |
| | Sidecar | 1 F. Camathias | FCS |
| | | 2 F. Scheidegger | BMW |
| | | 3 A. Birch | BMW |
| 1964 | Senior | 1 S. M. B. Hailwood | MV |
| | | 2 D. Minter | Norton |
| | | 3 F. Stevens | Matchless |
| | Junior | 1 J. Redman | Honda |
| | | 2 P. W. Read | AJS |
| | | 3 M. A. Duff | AJS |
| | Lightweight 250 cc | 1 J. Redman | Honda |
| | | 2 A. Shepherd | MZ |
| | | 3 A. Pagani | Paton |
| | Lightweight 125 cc | 1 L. Taveri | Honda |
| | | 2 J. Redman | Honda |
| | | 3 R. Bryans | Honda |
| | 50 cc | 1 H. R. Anderson | Suzuki |
| | | 2 R. Bryans | Honda |
| | | 3 I. Morishita | Suzuki |
| | Sidecar | 1 M. Deubel | BMW |
| | | 2 C. Seeley | FCSB |
| | | 3 G. Auerbacher | BMW |
| 1965 | Senior | 1 S. M. B. Hailwood | MV |
| | | 2 J. Dunphy | Norton |
| | | 3 M. Duff | Matchless |
| | Junior | 1 J. Redman | Honda |
| | | 2 P. W. Read | Yamaha |
| | | 3 G. Agostini | MV |

| Year | Class | Rider | Machine |
|------|-------|-------|---------|
| | Light-<br>weight<br>250 cc | 1 J. Redman<br>2 M. Duff<br>3 F. Perris | Honda<br>Yamaha<br>Suzuki |
| | Light-<br>weight<br>125 cc | 1 P. W. Read<br>2 L. Taveri<br>3 M. Duff | Yamaha<br>Honda<br>Yamaha |
| | 50 cc | 1 L. Taveri<br>2 H. R. Anderson<br>3 E. Degner | Honda<br>Suzuki<br>Suzuki |
| | Sidecar | 1 M. Deubel<br>2 F. Scheidegger<br>3 G. Auerbacher | BMW<br>BMW<br>BMW |
| 1966 | Senior | 1 S. M. B. Hailwood<br>2 G. Agostini<br>3 C. R. Conn | Honda<br>MV<br>Norton |
| | Junior | 1 G. Agostini<br>2 P. J. Williams<br>3 C. R. Conn | MV<br>AJS<br>Norton |
| | Light-<br>weight<br>250 cc | 1 S. M. B. Hailwood<br>2 L. S. Graham<br>3 P. G. Inchley | Honda<br>Honda<br>Villiers |
| | Light-<br>weight<br>125 cc | 1 W. Ivy<br>2 P. W. Read<br>3 H. R. Anderson | Yamaha<br>Yamaha<br>Suzuki |
| | 50 cc | 1 R. Bryans<br>2 L. Taveri<br>3 H. R. Anderson | Honda<br>Honda<br>Suzuki |
| | Sidecar | 1 F. Scheidegger<br>2 M. Deubel<br>3 G. Auerbacher | BMW<br>BMW<br>BMW |
| 1967 | Senior | 1 S. M. B. Hailwood<br>2 P. J. Williams<br>3 S. Spencer | Honda<br>Matchless<br>Lancefield/Norton |
| | Junior | 1 S. M. B. Hailwood<br>2 G. Agostini<br>3 D. Woodman | Honda<br>MV<br>MZ |
| | Light-<br>weight<br>250 cc | 1 S. M. B. Hailwood<br>2 P. W. Read<br>3 R. Bryans | Honda<br>Yamaha<br>Honda |
| | Light-<br>weight<br>125 cc | 1 P. W. Read<br>2 S. Graham<br>3 A. Motohashi | Yamaha<br>Suzuki<br>Yamaha |
| | 50 cc | 1 S. Graham<br>2 H. Anscheidt<br>3 T. Robb | Suzuki<br>Suzuki<br>Suzuki |
| | Sidecar | 1 S. Schauzu<br>2 K. Enders<br>3 C. Seeley | BMW<br>BMW<br>BMW |

| Year | Class | Rider | Machine |
|------|-------|-------|---------|
| 1968 | Senior | 1 G. Agostini | MV |
| | | 2 B. A. Ball | Seeley |
| | | 3 B. J. Randle | Petty/Norton |
| | Junior | 1 G. Agostini | MV |
| | | 2 R. Pasolini | Benelli |
| | | 3 W. A. Smith | Honda |
| | Lightweight 250 cc | 1 W. D. Ivy | Yamaha |
| | | 2 R. Pasolini | Benelli |
| | | 3 H. Rosner | MZ |
| | Lightweight 125 cc | 1 P. W. Read | Yamaha |
| | | 2 W. D. Ivy | Yamaha |
| | | 3 K. Carruthers | Honda |
| | 50 cc | 1 B. Smith | Derbi |
| | | 2 C. M. Walpole | Honda |
| | | 3 E. C. Griffiths | Honda |
| | Sidecar (500 cc) | 1 S. Schauzu | BMW |
| | | 2 J. Attenburger | BMW |
| | | 3 H. Luthringshauser | BMW |
| | Sidecar (750 cc) | 1 T. Vinnicombe | BSA |
| | | 2 N. Hanks | BSA |
| | | 3 P. Brown | BSA |
| 1969 | Senior | 1 G. Agostini | MV |
| | | 2 A. J. Barnett | Kirby Mettise |
| | | 3 T. Dickie | Seeley |
| | Junior | 1 G. Agostini | MV |
| | | 2 B. Steenson | Aermacchi |
| | | 3 J. Findlay | Aermacchi |
| | Lightweight 250 cc | 1 K. Carruthers | Benelli |
| | | 2 F. B. Perris | Crooks Suzuki |
| | | 3 S. Hennero | Ossa |
| | Lightweight 125 cc | 1 D. A. Simmonds | Kawasaki |
| | | 2 K. Carruthers | Aermacchi |
| | | 3 R. J. G. Dickenson | Honda |
| | Sidecar (500 cc) | 1 K. Enders | BMW |
| | | 2 S. Schauzu | BMW |
| | | 3 H. Fath | URS |
| | (750 cc) | 1 S. Schauzu | BMW |
| | | 2 P. M. Brown | BSA |
| | | 3 L. W. Currie | LWC |

# Bibliography

*The Book of Motor Cycle Racing*. Edited by Peter Carrick (Stanley Paul)
*Hailwood*. Mike Hailwood (Cassell)
*Motor Cycle Racing*. Peter Carrick (Paul Hamlyn)
*Motor Cycling Today*. Bob McIntyre (Arthur Barker)
*Prince of Speed*. Phil Read (Arthur Barker)
*Racing all my Life*. Derek Minter (Arthur Barker)
*TT Races*. Edited by Peter Arnold (Shell Mex & BP Ltd)
*Wheels of Fortune*. Jim Redman (Stanley Paul)

# Index